UNVEILING *The* MAN *of* SIN

Dr. Joe VanKoevering

UNVEILING THE MAN OF SIN
Copyright © 2007
Dr. Joe VanKoevering

God's News Publishing
P. O. Box 10475
St. Petersburg, FL 33733

ISBN Number: 978-0-9787049-5-7

All scripture references are taken from the King James Version of the Bible, unless otherwise noted.

Printed in the United States of America.

TABLE OF CONTENTS

PREFACE

Dear Reader,

You are about to read the most important book I have ever written. It will, without question, be the most controversial book that I ever write. For within its pages, I will not only present many important Biblical keys to identify the coming Antichrist...I will also give you a name – the name of a most unique man that I have tracked for over four years, that I believe could very well be "the man"!

I seek not to win an argument, nor to convince everyone, regarding what I present in this book. I merely challenge you to do as I have done. All my documentation within this message is part of the "public domain". You examine as I have, the very words, actions and intensions of this very unique man that I identify within this book. Compare them with the Scriptures themselves, and you discern for yourself.

In fact I challenge you to study it all yourself, and <u>try</u> to prove me wrong. Do me a favor, and <u>try</u> to prove me wrong, because in so doing, you will <u>then</u> have to see what I have seen. You will have to read what I have read, and then you will know what I now know, that there is no other man in the earth today as uniquely born, placed, positioned and motivated, than this one man, to potentially fulfill all the Bible prophesies concerning the coming...Man of Sin.

Dr. Joe VanKoevering

DEDICATION

I want to dedicate this book to all those people who care enough about the signs of the end-times who take the time to devour and study the prophetic scriptures so they can be informed of what exactly will transpire just before the soon return of Jesus Christ for His bride, the Church.

ACKNOWLEDGEMENT

I want to thank Marcus Bodie, for his exhaustive research, which greatly assisted in the completion of this work. I thank God that He brought this young man into my life. He has been like a son in the Gospel. I know that the Lord has called him to do great things for the Kingdom.

I also want to thank my wife, Kaye, God's News Board Member, Rev. Bob Armstrong, Debbie Brown, Mike Scott and Brenda Denski for their compilation and editing work, to help make this book possible.

I want to thank a very special couple, Rev. Ed and Veda Houze for their confidence in me and seed faith that began this work.

FOREWORD

In an era of "political correctness," when many are intimidated into keeping their true feelings under wraps, it is refreshing to find someone who says what they mean and means what they say. That is one of the things I have always admired about my good friend Joe VanKoevering. He possesses a sincere passion for the things of God and boldly, and yes, lovingly shares those convictions with tens of thousands every week via the God's News television ministry. Without a doubt, he is a vessel our Heavenly Father has raised up in these last days to be a "voice in the wilderness." In keeping with his determination to share his thoughts with all who will hear, Joe has provided the Body of Messiah with the book you now hold in your hand - *Unveiling the Man of Sin*.

There is a growing sentiment among a fair number of Bible students, myself included, that many of the long-held ideas about the end times and, specifically, the coming Antichrist are beginning to crumble under the weight of mounting evidence to the contrary. Thankfully, Joe has documented much of that evidence in this book and, I might add, in grand detail. So, if you were expecting a study on prophecy that marches in step with the thousands of non-descript prophecy books out there, you are out of luck. If on the other hand, you are willing to allow your preconceived notions to be challenged by Joe VanKoevering's latest work, you are in for a real treat.

Beyond raising questions about traditional eschatology pertaining to the Antichrist, Joe goes one step further. In *Unveiling the Man of Sin*, Joe systematically details astonishing information on an emerging personality in the geo-political arena who Joe then compares with the Biblical profile of Antichrist. The comparison is startling to say the least. I must say that Joe's argument concerning this person is, if nothing more, intriguing and thought provoking. That, in itself, is highly important because, in a day when so many want others to do the thinking for them, we need to be challenged once again to study and show ourselves approved unto God, rightly dividing the word of truth (2 Timothy 2:15). If in the end you disagree with some of his conclusions, so be it; but no serious Bible student can ignore the overwhelming evidence Joe's research has yielded that identifies the "multitude" from which the Antichrist arises.

I trust that you will enjoy this book, as I have, and be inspired to study the Scripture more diligently yourself. Furthermore, I hope that you will be motivated, as I am, to support with prayer and encouragement those servants of God who say what they mean and mean what they say.

Blessings,

Bill Cloud
Shoreshim Ministries, Cleveland TN

INTRODUCTION

2 Thessalonians 2:3-12(KJV) reads, *"Let no man deceive you by any means: for that day shall not come, except there come a falling away first, and that **Man of Sin be revealed**, the son of perdition; who opposeth and exalteth himself above all that is called God, or that is worshipped; so that he as God sitteth in the temple of God, shewing himself that he is God. Remember ye not, that, when I was yet with you, I told you these things? And now ye know what withholdeth that he might be revealed in his time. For the mystery of iniquity doth already work: only he who now letteth will let, until he be taken out of the way."*

"And then shall that Wicked <u>be revealed</u>, whom the Lord shall consume with the spirit of his mouth, and shall destroy with the brightness of His coming: even him, whose coming is after the working of Satan with all power and signs and lying wonders, and with all deceivableness of unrighteousness in them that perish; because they received not the love of the truth, that they might be saved. And for this cause God shall send them strong delusion, that they should believe a lie: that they all might be damned who believed not the truth, but had pleasure in unrighteousness."

Men have attempted to identify this Man of Sin throughout church history. Many years ago, they began to declare that Nero was the Antichrist. Then, of course, in more modern times, Adolph Hitler was thought to be the Antichrist. John F. Kennedy was the Antichrist for a while. Then Henry Kissinger became the Antichrist. In recent years, King Juan Carlos has been labeled as the

Antichrist. Yasser Arafat – he was a candidate for a while. Even President William Jefferson Clinton was presented at the International Prophecy Conference for many years by a particular speaker that he could be the Antichrist; as well as many others.

Perhaps the time has now come, however, that his true identity will be <u>revealed</u>.

"Surely the Lord GOD will do nothing, but He revealeth His secret unto his servants, the prophets." – Amos 3:7

God has given His people many names, indicators and facts about the identity of this Man of Sin. Prophetic teachers throughout church history have studied these Bible truths and these Scriptural indicators, knowing that a day would come when this Man of Sin would appear on the scene.

Surely this is the season and the generation when God will give His servants, the prophets, eyes to see what He has placed within the Holy Scriptures all along! Daniel was told that the words were not for now, that his words concerning the end of time and the revealing of the Man of Sin were to be closed up and "sealed" until the "time of the end." (Daniel 12:9)

Is it possible to know the identity of the Antichrist?

Some will say, "No;" but the Lord may be saying, "Now is the time!"

CHAPTER 1

Who Was The First Terrorist?

Today, the world is involved with a "war on terror". Those who study the Bible, however, know that the "real" war began long ago and the original "terrorist" is none other than Satan.

"Thou hast been in Eden the garden of God; every precious stone was thy covering, the sardius, topaz, and the diamond, the beryl, the onyx, and the jasper, the sapphire, the emerald, and the carbuncle, and gold: the workmanship of thy tabrets and of thy pipes was prepared in thee in the day that thou wast created. Thou art the anointed cherub that covereth; and I have set thee so: thou wast upon the holy mountain of God; thou hast walked up and down in the midst of the stones of fire. Thou wast perfect in thy ways from the day that thou wast created, till iniquity was found in thee. By the multitude of thy merchandise they have filled the midst of thee with violence, and thou hast sinned: therefore I will cast thee as profane out of the mountain of God: and I will destroy thee, O covering cherub, from the midst of the stones of fire. Thine heart was lifted up because of thy beauty, thou hast corrupted thy wisdom by reason of thy brightness: I will cast thee to the ground, I will lay thee before kings, that they may behold thee. Thou hast defiled thy sanctuaries by the multitude of thine iniquities, by the iniquity of thy traffic; therefore will I bring forth a fire from the midst of thee, it shall devour thee, and I will bring thee to ashes upon the earth in the sight of

*all them that behold thee. All they that know thee among the people shall be astonished at thee: thou shalt be a **terror**, and never shalt thou be any more."* – Ezekiel 28:13-19

Some scholars claim that this passage refers only to the King of Tyrus and not to Satan, but consider this description:

1. He had been in Eden (Genesis 3:1-17), where he tempted Adam and Eve, as an "angel of light" (2 Corinthians 11:14), the "shining one" (which is what "serpent" signifies)

2. His appearance and attire were bedecked with multi-colored jewels and gold of indescribable splendor.

3. His supernatural instruments included tabrets or timbrels (percussion instruments) probably indicating his immense musical ability.

4. He was an especially created being.

5. Only angelic beings are so designated in Scripture.

6. He was present with God.

7. He walked in the midst of "the stones of fire".

8. As a created being he was perfect until his fall. (See Isaiah 14:12-15, where he is called Lucifer meaning "light bearer").

The spirit of "terror" which is manifest in the world today, also known as "radical Islam" is merely the spirit of Lucifer himself, the original terrorist!

"How art thou fallen from heaven, O Lucifer, son of the morning! how art thou cut down to the ground, which didst weaken the nations!" – *Isaiah 14:12*

The Hebrew text for the word "Lucifer" in Isaiah 14:12 is "*Hilal ben Sahar.*"

Hilal also means "the brightness" and in Aramaic/Arabic it means "Crescent Moon." When we study these two words, "Hilal" and "Sahar," we find interesting refinements.

"Helel, or Heylel (morning star) have possible links with Akkadian elletu (Ishtar) and Arabic hilal (new moon)." [1]

"The worship of the moon is also attested to by proper names of people such as Hilal, a crescent; Qamar, a moon; and so on." [2]

"Hilal" means "the shining one" in Hebrew and Arabic, and in Ethiopian it means "Moon-crescent." He is a Moon-god. [3]

"Sahar" or "Shahar" is Hebrew for dawn or morning star. The two combined make up his symbol—crescent moon and star.

Walid Shoebat, in his outstanding book, <u>Why I Left Jihad</u>, p. 272, writes, "Islam is simply a revival of a Babylonian religion. The Moon god with the crescent moon and star symbol originated in Babylon (Iraq) and was one of the 360 idols in the Kaaba (Mecca) before Muhammad destroyed them. In Babylon, the Moon god was called 'Sin.'"

Dr. Arthur Jeffrey, professor of Islamic and Middle East Studies, one of the world's foremost scholars on Islam, said that the name "Allah," and its feminine form, "Allat," were well known in pre-Islamic Arabia and were found in inscriptions uncovered in North Africa: it "is a proper name applicable only to their peculiar god."

"Allah is a pre-Islamic name…corresponding to the Babylonian god known as Bel." "Bel" means "lord" and this is a title of reverence to the Moon-god "Sin."

"And the name *Sanballat the Araba* is a derivative of two words, the Sin (Moon-god), and Allat, the feminine of Allah, one of his three daughters. This shows that such names existed way before Muhammad, just as his father's name, Abd-Allah, meant "slave of Allah," the Moon-god. [4]

Walid Shoebat says, "The worship of the Moon-god came from Ur of the Chaldees in Babylon. Abraham is the first to mention it in his account of his journey in Genesis 12:1."

"Now the LORD had said unto Abram, Get thee out of thy country, and from thy kindred, and from thy father's house, unto a land that I will shew thee:" – *Genesis 12:1*

"In Surah 106, the Quran commanded Quays, Muhammad's clan, to 'worship the Lord of this shrine' (i.e., the Kabana) which can mean only the Moon-god. It is only after this Surah was revealed that Muhammad came back to destroy the idols in the Kabana and fight the people that refused to accept his status as prophet." [5]

The conclusion is that Satan, himself, the original terrorist, birthed and authored the religion of Islam under the name of "Allah". Ask yourself then, how will the coming Antichrist, by the influence and power of Satan, attempt to "rule the world"?

Surely this false religious system, with its false "Holy" book, carrying the "spirit of terror" itself must NOT be overlooked.

CHAPTER 2

Antichrist – Jew Or Gentile?

Many Bible scholars are mistaken about one of the attributes of the Antichrist. It has long been taught by many good men that the False Messiah will be Jewish. The main pretext for this theory is found again within the Book of Daniel.

"He should regard neither the God of his fathers…"
– Daniel 11:37

This has been taken to mean that the Antichrist will be a Jew that rejects Yahweh. But the word used for "God" is Elohim, and therefore could refer to any deity, any "god" true or false. In fact, looking at the scriptural evidence, it becomes apparent that the Man of Sin must indeed be a Gentile, concluding as it were the "times of the Gentiles" called for in Luke 21:24.

And they shall fall by the edge of the sword, and shall be led away captive into all nations: and Jerusalem shall be trodden down of the Gentiles, until the times of the Gentiles be fulfilled. – *Luke 21:24*

What do the real scholars say?

Dr. Arnold Fruchtenbaum, in his book entitled, "The Footsteps of the Messiah", says,

"The very fact that the plural form of the word 'God' is used in a context where the singular is found in the majority of cases makes this a reference to the heathen deities and not a reference to the God of Israel." He goes on to say, *"Further evidence that the King James Version is incorrect in its translation here is seen in the fact that almost all other English translations, both from Jewish and non-Jewish sources, have rendered the word for 'God' in the plural."*

Dr. Fruchtenbaum sums up his premise with this powerful statement: *"All this evidence shows that Daniel 11:37, the chief argument used by proponents that the antichrist is to be a Jew, gives no validity to this belief."* [6]

Let's now consider the conclusions of Dr. John Walvoord.

In his commentary on Daniel he makes this statement about explaining Daniel 11:37: *"One of the more important arguments supporting the conclusion that this king is a Jew is found in the opening phrase of verse 37: 'neither shall he regard the God of his fathers.' as Gaebelein states."*

"The king,' antichrist, 'shall not regard the God of his fathers.' Here his Jewish decent becomes evident. It is a Jewish phrase, 'the God of his fathers', and beside this, to establish his fraudulent claim to be the King Messiah, he must be a Jew.'"

But then says this, *"Gaebelein and others upholding this view, however, overlook a most decisive fact that the word for 'God' here is Elohim, a name for God in general, applying both to the true God and to false gods."*

He continues, *"If the expression had been the usual one when referring to the God of Israel, the Jehovah of his fathers, the identification would be unmistakable. Very frequently in Scripture, the God of Israel is described as Jehovah, 'the Lord God' of their fathers. Although Daniel uses 'God (Elohim) of my fathers' in Daniel 2:23 in view of this common usage elsewhere in Scripture, for Daniel to omit the word Jehovah or Lord, in a passage where a specific name for the God of Israel would be necessary, becomes 'significant'."*

He concludes, *"The expression should be rendered, 'the gods of his fathers,' that is, any god, as most revisions translate it. In keeping with the blasphemous character of this king who magnifies himself above every god, he disregards whatever deities his fathers worshipped. In keeping with the general word for god, Elohim, the expression, 'the gods of his fathers,' becomes a general reference to any deities, whether pagan or true God."* [7]

What's the conclusion?

The Man of Sin cannot be a Jew!

In fact he <u>must</u> be a <u>Gentile</u>.

Again, I go to <u>"The Footsteps of the Messiah"</u>, written by Dr. Arnold Fruchtenbaum, and he proves the premise that the Antichrist will be a Gentile, based upon a threefold argument. Here's his argument:

Number one: Biblical **typology**. He refers to Antiochus Epiphanies. Antiochus Epiphanies is believed, by every prophecy preacher that I admire, to be a type of the Antichrist. He wasn't a Jew. He was a Gentile. So Biblical typology indicates that the coming Man of Sin must be a Gentile.

Secondly: Biblical **imagery**. The beast arises out of the sea in Revelation 13. Do you know the word "sea" always represents the Gentile nations every single time it's found within the prophetic writings?

Thirdly: Fruchtenbaum's argument is the **nature** of the times of the Gentiles. The Antichrist is the final ruler of the times of the Gentiles. To say that the Antichrist is to be a Jew contradicts the very nature of the times of the Gentiles. Fruchtenbaum boldly states, "A Jew heading up the final world throne of Gentile power is an impossible postulation." [8]

Quoting Walid Shoebat's book, <u>Why I Left Jihad</u>, *"The claim of a Jewish Antichrist can have no validity, since the Antichrist comes to destroy Israel. Further, Jews worship the one true God of the Bible. The theory of a Jewish Antichrist was spawned by anti-Semitic Christendom."*

"The issue of Father and Son is actually not an issue at all in Hinduism, Buddhism, or other religions. Among all world religions, only the tenets of Islam deny the father and the Son. In fact, if you ask Muslims why they reject Christianity, they will happily tell you that God is not the Father of Jesus, God never became flesh, God does not have a Son, and Jesus was never crucified and did not rise from the dead. These are the leading arguments expressed in the Quran and the most frequently voiced by Muslims." [9]

Where does the word "Antichrist" come from?

Vines' Greek dictionary comments on this word, *"By combining the two words anti and Christ, it can mean one who assumes the guise of Christ, or opposes Christ."* [10]

Thusly, the Antichrist is one who is against Christ.

The word Antichrist was used by the Apostle John, who wrote John's Gospel, I, II and III John, and the Book of Revelation. The word itself, "Antichrist" can be found only in his writings.

He used the word Antichrist in four scriptures:

"Little children, it is the last time: and as ye have heard that antichrist shall come, even now are there many antichrists; whereby we know that it is the last time." (1 John 2:18)

"Who is a liar but he that denieth that Jesus is the Christ? He is antichrist, that denieth the Father and the son." (1 John 2:22)

"And every spirit that confesseth not that Jesus Christ

is come in the flesh is not of God: and this is the spirit of antichrist, whereof ye have heard that it should come; and even now is it in the world." (1 John 4:3)

"For many deceivers are entered into the world, who confess not that Jesus Christ is come in the flesh. This is a deceiver and an antichrist." (2 John 1:7)

Many say that the Antichrist is only a spirit. However, Antichrist is **BOTH** a spirit and a future person!

In the early church, some denied the divinity of Christ and had the "Antichrist spirit". Scriptures tell us that in the last days, the MAN OF SIN will be revealed, the "son of perdition".

"Let no man deceive you by any means: for that day shall not come, except there come a falling away first, and that man of sin be revealed, the son of perdition; who opposeth and exalteth himself above all that is called God, or that is worshipped; so that he as God sitteth in the temple of God, shewing himself that he is God."
– 2 Thessalonians 2:3-4

When one studies the Greek of the word in 2 John 1:7, *ho antichristos,* we find that it means "**the** antichrist". This refers to a very specific person. The Antichrist refers to a specific person to come in the very near future.

Let's look at 1 John 2:22: "Who is a liar but he that denieth that Jesus is the Christ? He is antichrist, that denieth the Father and the Son." – 1 John 2:22

The Antichrist denies the deity of Christ, and that Jesus Christ is the Son of God, and the relationship between the father and the Son. We find that there was spiritual conflict in those days, as there will be in the future in the land of Israel, over the person of Jesus Christ.

The fundamental difference between the Muslim faith and Christianity is that the Muslims believe that Jesus Christ was ONE of the prophets of Allah. We believe, of course, that Jesus Christ is the Son of the living and true God.

Evidence that the Antichrist is a mortal man and not just an evil spirit can be viewed in light of other New Testament passages that make use of personal pronouns. Evangelical scholars point to the following passages that reveal important details about this future world dictator. In each case, he is identified with the use of a masculine pronoun:

- The Antichrist is called "the man of sin," "the son of perdition" (2 Thessalonians 2:3).
- "He as God sitteth in the temple of God, showing himself that he is God" (verse 4).
- He will "be revealed in his time" (verse 6).
- The dragon gave him his power, and his seat, and great authority (Revelation 13:2).
- Who is able to make war with him? And there was given unto him a mouth speaking great things and

blasphemies; and power was given unto him to continue forty and two months (verses 4, 5).
• It was given unto him to make war (verse 7). [11]

DNA SAYS AN ASSYRIAN

Before 608 B.C., ancient Assyria occupied the same geographic area as Babylon. Isaiah's words may identify the Antichrist as "the Assyrian" because of his future role in Babylon.

"Therefore thus saith the Lord GOD of hosts, O my people that dwellest in Zion, be not afraid of ***the Assyrian***: he shall smite thee with a rod, and shall lift up his staff against thee, after the manner of Egypt." – Isaiah 10:24

An interesting DNA study is available from a renowned geneticist. The entire study is most informative on many levels and is worth reading. See www.assyrianfoundation. org/genetics.

The authors of the book <u>The History and Geography of Human Genes</u>, published in 1994, took on the monumental task of analyzing the vast number of research articles written about genetic properties of different human populations. The senior author, Professor L.L. Cavalli-Sforza, Professor of Genetics at Stanford University, is considered one of the preeminent human population geneticists in the world, a field that he has been working in for over forty years. After eight years of collecting this massive information, the authors spent several more years doing the genetic and statistical analyses using genetic variations in the entire human population of the world and, from that information, to trace the origin and migration of modern humans to their present locations on the planet.

The American Journal of Human Genetics stated, "This book represents a landmark in biology. There is nothing of its kind. It represents an essential historical source for all human biologists."

The closest genetic relationship of the Assyrians is with the native populations of Jordan and Iraq. In point of fact, however, all of the seven populations of interest are quite close to each other. There are no wide separations between any of them. This despite the fact that they contain members of three major language families: Indo-European (Iranian, Kurdish), Turkic (Turkish), and Semitic (Iraqi, Jordanian, Lebanese – Arabic; Assyrian – Aramaic). As the authors state, "In spite of the complex history of the Middle East and the great number of internal group migrations revealed by history, as well as the mosaic of cultures and languages, the region is relatively homogeneous (genetically)." [12]

There was an "extremely close affinity of Jewish and non-Jewish Middle Eastern populations (Palestinians, Syrians, Lebaneze, Druze, Saudi Arabians) observed that supports the hypothesis of a common Middle Eastern origin" of these populations dating back about 4,000 years.

The differences between the populations were not statistically significant, demonstrating once again the close genetic relationship of Middle Eastern populations to each other.

The results of these scientific studies lead to the startling realization that Turks, Iranians, Kurds, Iraqis, Jordanians, Lebanese are more closely related genetically to Assyrians than they are to other members of their own respective language families in Asia. These seven groups (and Jews) are genetically close.

What may one conclude from such a study?

Jordanians and Iraqis are closely related and the most closely related genetically to the modern Assyrians, (lending credibility to our hypothesis that the Assyrian Antichrist will come from Jordan/Iraq). However, there is a lot more forthcoming in this region. One must keep in mind that traditionally the Assyrians have been persecuted by the Islamists and many of them are Christians, in fact, many of them were the "original" Christians. [13]

CHAPTER 3

The Myth Of The European Man Of Sin

Many prophecy writers boldly state, "The Antichrist must come from Europe." However, upon close examination, is this widely held view actively supported by the scriptures?

The logical argument is in Daniel 9, the "people of the prince who is to come," speaks of a Roman Antichrist, and since Titus is the fulfillment, then it must be a revived Roman Empire from Europe. Since Europe is in the West, then the Antichrist must be a western leader, probably himself from Rome.

Yet, what many fail to see, is that this traditional interpretation forces a contradiction – and we know that there are no contradictions in the Bible. When one properly interprets Daniel chapter 7 and 8, one must conclude that the Antichrist <u>CANNOT</u> be from Western Europe.

In Daniel 8 and 11, the Antichrist is seen rising up in one of the four regions formed by the splintering of Alexander's Greek Empire (little horn).

Daniel continued to write about the area from which the Antichrist will arise. The Babylonian Empire fell into the hands of the Medes and Persians. The Babylonians and the Media-Persians ruled from Babylon during the time of the prophet Daniel.

Eventually, the Persian Empire fell into the hands of Alexander the Great, the leader of the Grecian Empire, which was represented by the symbol of a ram, or male goat:

"And the rough goat is the king of Grecia: and the great horn that is between his eyes is the first king."
– Daniel 8:21

Daniel predicted that the Grecian Empire be divided into four divisions. The horn, or kingdom, of the goat would divide into four regions:

"Therefore the he goat waxed very great: and when he was strong, the great horn was broken; and for it came up four notable ones toward the four winds of heaven"
– Daniel 8:8

This prophecy has been accurately fulfilled and has caused many doubters to suggest that a 'latter Daniel' wrote the book of Daniel. Yet, no such evidence can be found to support this, and the unearthing of the Book of Daniel among the Dead Sea Scrolls has provided much evidence that the book is the prophetic scripture.

Alexander the Great, the head of the Grecian Empire, died drunk in Babylon. His kingdom was divided among his four main generals, or as Daniel alludes to the "four winds" (north, east, south, and west). Here are the names of Alexander's four generals who took possession of the four main regions of the Grecian Empire:

1. <u>General Cassander</u> took Greece, Macedon, and the western part, which was the Greek/Macedonian region (Macedonia is a Muslim majority state today).

2. <u>General Lysimachus</u> took Turkey, Thrace and the northern part of the empire. The Thracia/Turkey region (Bulgaria and Turkey today) was later called the Byzantine Empire, which is Muslim today.

3. <u>General Seleucus</u> took Babylon, Syria, Iran, Iraq and the eastern part. The Babylonian/Persian region, including Southern Russia, Afghanistan, Iran, Syria, Lebanon, Arabia and all the coastland to the city of Tyre, Lebanon. This region was known as the Seleucid Dynasty. Most of all these countries are Muslim today.

4. <u>General Ptolemy</u> took Egypt and the southern part of the empire. The whole of Egypt, which in prophecy includes Libya and the Nubians and are Muslim regions today.

Daniel makes it clear that the Antichrist, identified as the "little horn" in Daniel 7:8 and Daniel 8:9, would arise out of **one** of these four regions of the Grecian Empire.

"And out of one of them came forth a little horn, which waxed exceeding great, toward the south, and toward the east, and toward the pleasant land." – Daniel 8:9

Daniel gives four choices for the rise of the world's final dictator: Egypt, Turkey, Greece, or the regions of Syria (and Iraq, which includes portions of ancient Babylon). This is highlighted again in Daniel 8:

"And the rough goat is the king of Grecia: and the great horn that is between his eyes is the first king. Now that being broken, whereas four stood up for it, four kingdoms shall stand up out of the nation, but not in his power." – Daniel 8:21, 22

This refers to the division of the kingdom after the death of Alexander the Great. The four choices we are given are:
1. Greece
2. Turkey
3. Syria/Babylon
4. Egypt

The Antichrist **must** come from one of those areas.

The future dictator will seize control of Egypt during his rule, so that eliminates Egypt. Turkey is the king of the north that will push against the Antichrist and his armies during the early part of the Tribulation, so that eliminates Turkey or Asia Minor. That only leaves two. The Antichrist is identified as the Assyrian, or (the Babylonian), instead of coming from Israel, the Antichrist will invade Israel in the middle of the Tribulation.

There are only four that it can be. It says he waxed great towards the south, towards the east, and towards the Pleasant land. When you look at it, it only leaves ancient Assyria. Stop looking at Rome. Rome is not even on the map.

If this kingdom waxes EXCEEDING GREAT, TOWARD THE SOUTH, EAST, and the PLEASANT LAND (Israel/Palestine), then follow me here. These directions point to three exclusive compass directions.

The kingdom is growing in THREE directions. If the kingdom was West of Israel, EAST and the PLEASANT LAND would be the same direction. Therefore, the kingdom is NOT west of Israel.

If the kingdom was North of Israel, the SOUTH and PLEASANT LAND would be redundant. Therefore, the kingdom is not north of Israel.

This leaves SOUTH of Israel and EAST of Israel as our two choices. We have to eliminate the SOUTH of Israel because the Antichrist attacks and conquers the king of the south – Egypt.

This leaves us with EAST of Israel as the place of the new "entity". **Jordan-Iraq is the place**. The United States policy in the Mideast is to build a central democratic state, which should eventually lead to a "free" and democratic group of nations that will presumably not support terrorism. Right or wrong, the Bush administration is conducting a war in Iraq for the very reason that they stated, "freeing" Iraq. Unknown to the Bush administration is the fact that they are building a "free" nation in the very center of the future Biblical kingdom of the Antichrist.

Iraq, ancient Babylon, the region taken by General Seleucus, **MUST** be where the "little horn" emerges from!

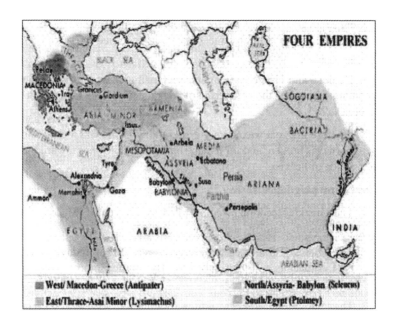

This map shows the four divisions of Alexander the Great's Grecian empire. Note that the only portion in the West is Greece and the rest of the divisions are all in the East. The three Eastern divisions are ALL Islamic nations today, which surround Israel!

CHAPTER 4

Insights From
The Book Of Beginnings

Often times people try to interpret "the end time" by merely going to the end of the Bible, namely the book of Revelation, and base their interpretations and conclusions SOLELY on what they find there. However, any true student of Bible prophecy knows, that nothing in the book of Revelation has its origin or beginning there. Everything within the book of Revelation began earlier, with the other books and prophetic writers of the Bible. If you fail to study the ENTIRE Bible, then the "final chapter" so to speak, will have little relevance and understanding.

It's time we, as students of Bible prophecy, placed proper weight of significance upon the "beginning of the book" namely the book of Genesis. I truly believe that God is showing those who "have ears to hear" in this hour, that everything about "the end" has already been hidden within the pages of "the beginning".

"Remember the former things of old: for I am God, and there is none else; I am God, and there is none like me. Declaring the end from the beginning, and from ancient times the things that are not yet done, saying, My counsel shall stand, and I will do all my pleasure" – Isaiah 46:9-10

I also believe that the entire story of Biblical history can be summed up and capsulated within one verse from Genesis.

"And I will put enmity between thee and the woman, and between thy seed and her seed; it shall bruise thy head, and thou shalt bruise his heel." – Genesis 3:15

All Bible scholars agree, that in this verse we find the very first prophecy of scripture, as Jesus Himself can be seen here, as the coming "seed of the woman". Yet also within this profound declaration, if time would allow, we could demonstrate how the entire "conflict" of the ages, is found here as well. God's "good seed" versus Satan's "bad seed" has created the history of mankind as God has brought His redemptive plan to bear in the earth. This "enmity" which began in the Garden of Eden, has NEVER been removed from the earth. And the final, culmination of all things, which is described in the book of Revelation, is actually the final manifestation of this very same "enmity!"

Just as God has His Seed in the earth, producing a harvest of His character and His righteousness; SO TOO does Satan have "his seed" in the earth, producing a harvest of his unholy character and his un-righteousness. The coming "man of sin" is merely the final manifestation of that original seed which desires to thwart, stop and oppose the seed of God! He will truly be the seed of the serpent!

If we will take the time to examine how it "all began" we

will invariably discover the hidden keys which will unveil how it will "all end." So let's examine it.

He is A MAN

Revelation reveals that the man of sin, will in fact be "A Man".

"Here is wisdom. Let him that hath under-standing count the number of the beast: for it is the number of a man; and his number is Six hundred three score and six." – Revelation 13:18

The spirit of Antichrist has been in the earth from the beginning, with demonstrations of enmity toward God and God's purposes in the earth. But the purpose of this very book, is to show that the "spirit" will manifest in "a man" at the end of this age. The question is, does God unveil the origin of this man in the book of beginnings, the book of Genesis?

The very first manifestation of the "enmity factor" between God's Seed and the seed of the serpent, was with the very first son, birthed by Eve, Cain.

"And Adam knew Eve his wife; and she conceived, and bare Cain, and said, I have gotten a man from the Lord." – Genesis 4:1

Please notice that phrase, "a man".

Cain was the "seed of the serpent" and demonstrated the serpent's character, as he eventually killed his brother Abel, because God rejected his offering, which was based upon his own merit rather than the blood covering which God had prescribed.

Cain became known as a "fugitive" and a "vagabond" in the earth (Genesis 4:12 & 14)

God had to put a "mark" on Cain, to make him separate and distinct among the people of the earth. (Genesis 4:15)

The name "Cain" itself, has the meaning from the original Hebrew language, of one who will "take and possess – against one's will." Abel's very blood cried out from the earth, as a testimony against Cain and his evil actions. (Genesis 4:10) We could say that Abel was the very first "martyr" slain for his faith in God!

One of Cain's descendants, known as Tubal-Cain (meaning "to proceed forth or from" Cain) is credited in scripture, as the first man to create and forge metal weapons, and <u>swords</u>! (Genesis 4:22)

Are you starting to see "the end" here in "the beginning"? We anticipate "A Man" who will come at the end, but we find God himself giving us the clues from the beginning, so as to help us identify him, before he actually comes.

In fact, God boldly tells us this, within the very text, but because we don't know the original language (Hebrew) we miss it, even when we read it. Notice verse 3 of Genesis chapter 4:

"And in the process of time, it came to pass, that Cain brought of the fruit of the ground an offering unto the Lord." – Genesis 4:3

The words translated "in the process of time" from the Hebrew, literally mean at the end of days! In other words, God was saying within this story, that it is prophetic! It has "hidden" meaning and application to <u>the very end of days</u>!

I am not the first Bible teacher to draw a comparison between Cain and coming man of sin, and the Antichrist spirit. One such scholar stated: " Thus the original rebel against God was Cain…He was, therefore, the original 'Beast' who thought to change times and laws." [14]

In fact, my good friend Bill Cloud has stated: "That the global aspirations of militant Islam is surfacing just now is, in my opinion no accident. It is in fact, a satanic response to what God has determined to do within His body…In essence, it boils down to this: there are two groups – those who have been marked by God as "Righteous," and those who have been marked by God as being the successors to Cain – the serpent's seed." [15]

The coming man of Sin will come forth as Cain!

The "Wild" Man

The next manifestation of the "serpent's seed" given to us within the book of Genesis is Ishmael. Before we look at this very important passage of scripture, let me remind you, that virtually all of the Arab world, and the originator of Islam itself Muhammad, are the clear descendants of this man Ishmael!

"And the angel of the Lord said unto her (Hagar), Behold, thou art with child, and shalt bear a son, and shalt call his name Ishmael; because the Lord hath heard her affliction. And he will be a wild man; his hand will be against every man, and every man's hand against him; and he shall dwell in the presence of all his brethren." – Genesis 16: 11-12

Please notice that important phrase, for we find it again, "A (wild) MAN." Only now, "the man" is given a further detailed distinction. He is a wild man! Other good translations, actually bring out what is found in the actual Hebrew, "a wild ass of a man!"

Hebrew scholars Keil and Delitzsch write about how accurately this metaphor describes the Arab people: "The figure of a wild ass, that wild and untamable animal, roaming at its will in the desert…depicts most aptly the Bedouin's boundless love of freedom as he rides about in the desert, spear in hand, upon his camel or his horse, hardy, frugal, reveling in the varied beauty of nature, and despising town life in every form." [16]

God poetically describes the nature of a wild ass in His challenge to Job: *"Who set the wild ass free? Who loosed the bonds of the swift ass, Whose home I have made the wilderness, And the barren land his dwelling? He scorns the tumult of the city; He does not heed the shouts of the driver. The range of the mountains is his pasture, And he searches after every green thing." Job 39:5-8 (from the Hebrew text)*

This perfectly describes the nature and characteristics of Ishmael, and his descendants, the Arabs. Like the donkeys of the wilderness, they fiercely love their freedom and independence. They have always had a warrior's temperament.

Now within this text from Genesis 16, once again there is "hidden" meaning. For within the original Hebrew language, we find further understanding. The Hebrew word for presence ("…and he shall dwell in the presence of all his brethren.") is the same word for FACE. Or rather, "he shall dwell in the face of his brethren." This very wording in the Hebrew means "to stand in defiant hostility toward!"

Some translations bring this out better than others. The New International Version for one, correctly expresses the true sense of it, "…and he will live in hostility toward all his brothers."

Here we clearly can identify, once again, the enmity which dwells between the seeds!

Ishmael grew to hate Isaac, the promised seed, and to this day demonstrates that hatred with defiant hostility against the true "Seed of God" the descendants of Isaac! At the end of days, another "wild man" will stand up in the earth, with hatred and defiant hostility, and seek to destroy his "brethren" the Hebrew people. Ask yourself then, from where will this "seed" spring forth from? Surely it MUST spring up from this same seed, this same man and these same people!

The coming man of sin will come forth as Ishmael!

A Hairy Hunter

No better example of the enmity between the seeds, can be found than with Esau and Jacob. In this account we see exactly how the "seed of the serpent" desires to respond to the promised seed of God. <u>He desires to take off his head</u>!

"And the LORD said unto her, Two nations are in thy womb, and two manner of people shall be separated from thy bowels; and the one people shall be stronger than the other people; and the elder shall serve the younger. And when her days to be delivered were fulfilled, behold, there were twins in her womb. And the first came out red, all over like an hairy garment; and they called his name Esau. And after that came his brother out, and his hand took hold on Esau's heel; and his name was called Jacob: and Isaac was threescore years old when she bare them. And the boys grew: and Esau was a cunning hunter, <u>a man</u> of the field; and Jacob was a plain man, dwelling in tents." – Genesis 25: 23-27

Notice, now for the third time, our all important identifying term, "A MAN!"

God tells us boldly that there where two nations within Rebekah's womb. The promise was passed down to Jacob, later to become Israel. Jacob's very name means "heel catcher." Why? Because, the "seed of the serpent" knows the prophecy given in Genesis 3:15, of the coming "seed of God" who will crush his head. In an attempt to turn the tables on God, the serpent seeks, once again, to violently destroy the promised seed before he is even born!

Jacob protects himself, and "his head" in order to even be born. This is once again a "prophetic picture" given to us, in the beginning, depicting what will come at the end!

The descendants of Esau are in every way the "seed of the serpent!" They will try to "take off the head's" of Jacob's descendants – Israel!

Once again, my dear friend Bill Cloud makes a significant observation concerning this in his excellent book, "Enmity Between the Seeds." I strongly recommend you acquire this very important book, and read it for yourself.

"Through the house of Esau, it appears that the Adversary was earnestly trying to fulfill his plan to destroy the Promised Seed. He tried with Cain. He probably tried with Ishmael. He tried harder with Esau, and he certainly attempted to destroy God's Promised One at Golgotha. And while that was his ultimate goal – to destroy the Messiah – the incident surrounding Jacob's birth and the subsequent hostility between he and his brother should not be underestimated, for it demonstrates the enemy's intense hatred for God's people ISRAEL."

"Why do you think that the nation of Israel and her descendants have always suffered at the hand of the oppressor? Put simply, the serpent wants to destroy Israel before his head is flattened, and that is why, I believe, Esau and his descendants after him sought and are presently seeking to destroy their brother Jacob – Israel." [17]

Clearly, a man is coming!

He will come forth as Esau! He will come forth as Cain, Ishmael and Esau! Hidden within the text of Genesis we discover this pattern, being given by God.

The "seed of the serpent" will manifest at <u>the end</u>, JUST AS IT DID IN THE BEGINNING!

CHAPTER 5

Spirit Of Islam Is The Spirit Of Antichrist

1 John Chapter 2 speaks of the Antichrist.

"Who is a liar but he that denieth that Jesus is the Christ? He is antichrist, that denieth the Father and the Son. Whosoever denieth the Son, the same hath not the Father: (but) he that acknowledgeth the Son hath the Father also." – 1 John 2:22-23

He goes on in chapter 4: "Beloved, believe not every spirit, but try the spirits whether they are of God: because many false prophets are gone out into the world. Hereby know ye the Spirit of God: Every spirit that confesseth that Jesus Christ is come in the flesh is of God: And every spirit that confesseth not that Jesus Christ is come in the flesh is not of God: and this is that spirit of antichrist..." – 1 John 4:1-3a

According to these words written by John, the Antichrist will:
1. Deny the deity of Jesus
2. Deny that Jesus Christ is the Son of God
3. Deny the relationship between the Father and the Son

As I have previously stated, the major rift between Islam and Christianity is the belief that Jesus was, Jesus is now, and Jesus will forever be the Son of the Living God. The basic tenet of Islam declares that God has no Son. Islam denies the relationship of Jesus and the Father. This is the spirit of Antichrist.

In my book, <u>The Church Under End Time Attack</u>, I write this, *"It's not politically correct, but I'm going to speak the truth. The spirit behind radical Islam is the spirit of Antichrist! Furthermore, should a Muslim come to power in the next few months or few years, gets the entire Muslim world united behind him in and effort to combat Christianity, including a concentrated effort to combat the nation of Israel, I'm here to tell you that person is the Antichrist."* [18]

I truly believe that whatever one can say about the "Antichrist spirit," we must all agree, that the spirit behind Islam in the earth today, surely is the greatest manifestation of this spirit.

Critics would contend that this fact, however, doesn't necessarily "prove" in and of itself, that the physical man who will emerge in the earth eventually as THE Antichrist, has to be Muslim.

Therefore, let's examine "additional" Biblical evidences that support our premise. When you look at the total picture, with each individual "piece" of a puzzle, as they join together, I believe you will then see a clearer and fuller "picture."

ABUSE OF WOMEN

"Neither shall he regard the God of his fathers, nor <u>the desire of women</u>, nor regard any god: for he shall magnify himself about all." – Daniel 11:37

Many preachers have speculated that the Antichrist may be homosexual. The term *no desire of women* infers his lack of interest in the opposite sex. While this scripture does not clearly state that this man will be openly gay, the fact is that if homosexuality is common in certain regions, it would not forbid this sexual orientation in the coming Antichrist.

However, a better rendering of these words could be "the abuse of women," or "the rights of women." Suddenly, the verse takes on a very different, and I believe, a more accurate interpretation.

In numerous Middle Eastern and Gulf nations, women are not treated with the admiration and self-esteem they would receive in the West. In most Islamic nations, women are forced to wear the traditional Arab and Islamic clothes (covering all but the eyes), and are often abused, manipulated and even dominated by their husbands.

Entire books have been recently written from women within the Muslim community, documenting the harsh abuse of women, and how Islam itself, inherently, carries within it the total disregard of women's rights.

The malicious and vindictive handling of women was seen during the Gulf War when Iraq invaded Kuwait. The Iraqi soldiers raped almost every woman they could find. Some were raped multiple times and were then murdered. These women were not Jews or Christians, but Muslims!

Islam denies rights to women. The Antichrist will have no regard for women's rights. Women will have no voice in his empire, just as they do not in Islam.

THE MARK OF THE BEAST: AN INSIGNIA OF SERVITUDE

*"And he causeth all, both small and great, rich and poor, free and bond, to receive **a mark** in their right hand, or in their foreheads: And that no man might buy or sell, save he that had the mark, or the name of the beast, or the number of his name. Here is wisdom. Let him that hath understanding count the number of the beast: for it is the number of a man; and his number is Six hundred threescore and six."* – Revelation 13:16-18

The characters chi xi stigma are not actually Greek characters at all, but rather a symbol that John saw and inscribed on the manuscript. Compare the "X" in the third line here.

46

With the next image, which is actually the Islamic symbol of two crossed swords.

The next word in the fragment appears to be "Allah" written vertically in Arabic script. It is impossible to know whether the scholars who copied the original text simply did not recognize the Arabic, and, in an attempt to make sense of it, inscribed what appears to be the Greek letter *Xi*. It is quite possible that John actually saw the mark of the beast – *Bism Allah*, which is translated "in the name of Allah" – and that he simply recorded it as accurately as he could.

Consider that the Greek word *Psephizo* can be translated "to decide" and that *Arithmos* can simply mean a "multitude." With this in mind, an alternative translation would read:

Here is wisdom. Let him that hath understanding decide (who) the multitude of the beast (is), for it is the multitude of a man (that is, Muhammad) and his multitude (are) *"In the Name of Allah."*

Compare this with the following passage concerning the multitude of the beast.

"And he saith unto me, the waters which thou sawest, where the whore sitteth, are people, and multitudes, and nations, and tongues."

The whore sitting on the beast controls the "multitudes," which are peoples and nations. [19]

Here, we see the three variations of the name of the beast: mark, name (title), or multitude (follower of this multitude).

The Greek word *charagma* used for "mark" is actually a "badge of servitude" or of allegiance and servanthood. <u>Strong's Hebrew Lexicon</u> defines *charagma* as "the mark stamped on the forehead or the right hand as the badge of the followers of the Antichrist." Note that the phrase "right arm" is from the Greek *dexios*, which could also be translated "right side."

Walid Shoebat, in his book, <u>WHY I LEFT JIHAD</u>, declares, "The Islamic Shahadatan is actually a declaration of allegiance and servitude to Allah and Muhammad; the inscription of this declaration is worn by millions on the forehead or right arm. It can be seen among Muslim demonstrators and jihadists. There is absolutely nothing in the text of Revelation 13 to suggest that followers of the Antichrist will be required to have a chip implanted on their foreheads or their arms/hands." [20]

BE-HEADING STILL COMMON IN ISLAMIC COUNTRIES

"And I saw thrones, and they sat upon them, and judgment was given unto them: and I saw the souls of them that were <u>beheaded</u> for the witness of Jesus, and for the word of God,

and which had not worshipped the beast, neither his image, neither had received his mark upon their foreheads, or in their hands; and they lived and reigned with Christ a thousand years." – Revelation 20:4

Who besides Muslims sees the killing of Jews and Christians as a religious obligation, as doing a service to God? Around the world, Muslims blow up embassies and other Western and Israeli targets in the name of Allah. Although the Roman Catholic Church, burdened with its own violent past, might be seen as the possible fulfillment of the harlot, the kingdom of the Antichrist practices beheading its enemies. Only in Islam is beheading a continuing practice.

The beheading of criminals with a sword or axe was common practice among ancient civilizations for thousands of years. This practice was widely used in Europe, Asia, and Africa – in both Muslim and non-Muslim nations – until the very early twentieth century. Only recently has the entire civilized world abandoned the practice of beheading. This barbarism is present <u>only</u> in the Muslim world – including Saudi Arabia, Qatar, Yemen, Iran, and until recently, Talibani Afghanistan. [21]

Jesus, Himself, speaking of the persecution that will come in the last days, namely upon the Jewish followers of God, seems to even identify the Islamic connection.

"They shall put you out of the synagogues: yea, the time cometh, that whosoever killeth you will think that he doeth

God service." – John 16:2

Ask yourself, what other false religious belief system, other than Islam, would consider it a "service unto God" (Allah) to take Believers (infidels) right out of their places of worship and kill them?

Ask yourself also, would a Jewish Antichrist seek to kill fellow Jews, and do so as a "service unto (a Jewish) God? Of course not! Jews don't desire to kill fellow Jews.

With everything I know and I have studied concerning Islam, I personally believe that Jesus, Himself, within this verse, is helping us to specifically identify this end-time spirit!

Islam persecutes the saints and institutes beheading as a form of punishment.

THE EUPHRATES CONNECTION

"Saying to the sixth angel which had the trumpet, Loose the four angels which are bound in <u>the great river Euphrates</u>. And the four angels were loosed, which were prepared for an hour, and a day, and a month, and a year, for to slay the third part of men. – Revelation 9:14, 15

The Tigris and Euphrates rivers divide Iran from Iraq. The Euphrates begins in Turkey not far from Mount Ararat. It travels through Turkey, Syria and Iraq, and empties into the Persian Gulf.

This river is the <u>only</u> river mentioned by name in prophecies related to the final days of the rule of the Beast kingdom. The old Roman Empire had the Euphrates as the eastern boundary.

Why is the emphasis on the Euphrates so important?

Ancient Babylon was built along the Euphrates. Baghdad, Iraq, is near the Tigris River, not far from the Euphrates. If the Euphrates dries up and a massive army marches across, they will march from the area of Iran, Afghanistan and Pakistan, countries that are located east of the Euphrates.

Iran, Afghanistan and Pakistan have millions of Islamic radicals, all promoting their obsessive program. The Antichrist will be "great toward the east" (Daniel 8:9), which includes these Islamic-controlled areas. Armies marching from the east would need to pass through Iraq, as they proceed into Israel and the valley of Megiddo.

Iraq has a tremendous prophetic history, second only to Israel. There is great spiritual and political importance in Iraq.

The Euphrates River is one more small "proof" of the Islamic connection!

CHAPTER 6

Who Is The Mahdi?

The president of Iran has been boldly proclaiming that the "Mahdi" is coming, "The restorer of religion and justice who will rule before the end of the world." Muslims have an eschatology just like we Christians do. They believe that the end of days is coming. They believe that they will win in the end. They believe that the whole world will be controlled and subjugated to Allah and his prophet Muhammad. Islamic writings boldly proclaim the Mahdi will come, but he's going to come with Jesus.

That's why a Muslim will actually say, "We believe what you Christians believe, that Jesus is coming back to earth." They want to make it sound like they believe the same things that we, as Christians, believe. However, their actual beliefs are dramatically different! Their concept of Jesus and His return is far different than what the Scripture teaches. The Jesus of Islam is a Muslim who will return and help convert the world to the Islamic religion.

Muslims believe they will one day control the entire world and that everyone will eventually become a Muslim. I was also disturbed to discover what most Muslims felt about Jews and the state of Israel, especially among those Muslims living in the Middle East.

The Shiites have a teaching called the Doctrine of the

Twelve. It states that after Mohammed, there were 11 caliphs. The 12th was the son of the 11th, and he disappeared when he was a young boy.

Since the graves of the other 11 are known and the grave of the 12th has never been discovered, the tradition states that the 12th caliph has been supernaturally protected by Allah for the past 1,200 years. Most say he is in a desert in Arabia. Still others believe he is being preserved in Iraq.

Since the disappearance of the 12th Imam in 878 A.D., Muslims have been expecting a final prophet to appear. He is called the Mahdi and will lead a last-days Islamic revival. This man, according to tradition, will be a military expert who will bring the world under the control of Islamic law and justice.

The Shiites, which is the more radical group, are placing high expectations upon the soon arrival of this prince who will conquer Israel and the West. Many will tell you that it won't be long now. This sect teaches that, at the end of days, the 12th Imam will reappear and become the final prophet of Islam. This man is recognized in the Islamic world as the Mahdi. [22]

An official state media website in Iran has posted a message heralding the coming of the Shiite messianic figure, Imam Mahdi, noting he could arrive with Jesus by the spring equinox.

"Imam Mahdi (may God hasten his reappearance) will

appear all of a sudden on the world scene with a voice from the skies announcing his reappearance at the holy Ka'ba in Mecca," the message says.

The Islamic Republic of Iran broadcasting website said in a program called "The World Toward Illumination," that the Mahdi will form an army to defeat the enemies of Islam in a series of apocalyptic battles, in which the Mahdi will overcome his archvillain in Jerusalem.

In a greeting to the world's Christians for the coming new year, Iranian President Mahmoud Ahmadinejad said he expects both Jesus and the Mahdi, to return and "wipe away oppression."

"I wish all the Christians a very happy new year and I wish to ask them a question as well," said Ahmadinejad, according to an Iranian Student News Agency cited by YnetNews.com.

"My one question to the Christians is: What would Jesus do if he were present in the world today? What would he do before some of the oppressive powers of the world who are in fact residing in Christian countries? Which powers would he revive and which of them would he destroy?" asked the Iranian leader.

All Iran is buzzing about the Mahdi, the 12th imam and the role Iran and Ahmadinejad are playing in his anticipated return. There's a new messiah hotline. There are news agencies especially devoted to the latest developments.

"People are anxious to know when and how he will rise; what they must do to receive this worldwide salvation," says Ali Lari, a cleric at the Bright Future Institute in Iran's religious center of Qom. "The timing is not clear, but the conditions are more specific," he adds. "There is a saying: "When the students are ready, the teacher will come." [23]

In a recent <u>NEWSWEEK</u> article, news flashes about the coming Mahdi in Iraq are spreading.

"Fighters repeatedly tapped into their radio frequency and repeated an ominous message, 'Imam Mahdi is coming! The return of the Mahdi – the 12th and last Shiite saint, who, believers say, vanished in the ninth century – signals the end of times."

"The two biggest players in the region are Moqtada al-Sadr's Mahdi Army and the Supreme Council for Islamic Revolution in Iraq, run by cleric Abdul Aziz al-Hakim."

"...In this chaotic environment, talk of the *dhuhoor*, or appearance of the Mahdi, has been growing. "The decrease of the things people need – electricity, water, a salary, peace of mind – makes them want to find something like a miracle," says Salama Khafaji, a former member of the Iraqi Governing Council from Najaf. Sadr has astutely tapped into this longing for a better world; loyalists have hinted that he may be the Mahdi himself. Fringe groups that take the Mahdi more literally – and that rail against a Shiite leadership who are doing nothing to hasten his return – are also growing, says Khafaji. "When you have the complete collapse of society is exactly when you get these pretenders who combine social anxiety, political frustration and fear with millenarian expectations," says Nasr. [24]

"The word Mahdi translates as 'the guided one.' The belief, especially among Shiites, is that the Mahdi will be guided so directly by Allah that he will be divinely protected from error and sin in all that he does. He will interpret Islam to all men and lead the final Islamic revolution that will convert the world to the religion of Islam. Shiites believe the Mahdi will be both a political and a military leader of great conquest.

There are numerous traditions concerning this mysterious person. The Islamic holy book, the Koran, has little to say concerning this man. Most traditions developed in the eighth century and beyond. While both the Sunni and the Shiite branches have a teaching on the Mahdi, the Shiites have the strongest teaching that he will appear near the end of the world.

What perhaps you have not known until now however, is that the Islamic writings themselves give us several key identifying characteristics, because the Islamic world and the world at large must be able to identify the Mahdi when he comes.

There are numerous, distinctive signs that identify the coming of the Mahdi:

1. His name will be "Muhammad ibn Hassan" (holy descendent of Muhammad), and he will trace his lineage as a direct descendant through Fatima, the daughter of Muhammad.
2. He will have the disposition of Mohammed.
3. His father and Mohammed's have the same name.
4. He will have a broad, bald forehead and a prominent pointed nose.
5. He will appear just before the end of the world, during a time of great difficulty.
6. He will convert the world to the Islamic faith.
7. The Mahdi will receive the pledge and support of the Iraqi people.
8. The Mahdi will spread justice and equity on the earth.
9. The Mahdi will rule over the Arabs for seven years.

As Muslims around the globe eagerly await the coming Mahdi, one national leader believes his "calling" from Allah is to "prepare the way" for the Mahdi's coming. His name is none other than the Iranian President Mahmoud Ahmadinejad.

MAHMOUD AHMADINEJAD

Iranian President Ahmadinejad's rhetoric about nuclear weapons is certainly troubling, but his most venomous statements have been directed toward Israel and the Jewish people. On October 26, 2005, at a conference titled, *"A World Without Zionism,"* Ahmadinejad addressed a gathering of about 4,000 students. Standing in front of a huge banner that read, "A World Without Zionism," he dropped several verbal bombshells: "They ask, 'Is it possible for us to witness a world without America and Zionism?' But you had best know that this slogan and this goal are altogether attainable, and surely can be achieved. This regime that is occupying Jerusalem must be wiped from the map."

The only bit of good news for Israel in these statements is that at least Ahmadinejad has recognized that Israel is "on the map." No Arab or Islamic nation up to this point has even recognized the existence of the Jewish state or included Israel on any map of the region.

Ahmadinejad has made a number of other aggressive, inflammatory, anti-Semitic statements.

"No doubt the new wave (of attacks) in Palestine will soon wipe off this disgraceful blot (Israel) from the face of the Islamic world."

"The establishment of the Zionist regime was a move by the world oppressor against the Islamic world."

"Palestine is the center of the final stages of the battle between Islam and arrogance."

"Anyone who signs a treaty with Israel means he has signed the surrender of the Muslim world."

"We say that this fake regime (Israel) cannot logically

continue to live."

And get this one: "Whether you like it or not, the Zionist regime is on the road to being eliminated."

These statements have met with universal condemnation by the West, but the nations of the Middle East have been strangely silent. Their silence is certainly indicative of their approval of his venomous anti-Semitism.

In the same vein as Hitler in his infamous *Mein Kampf*, Iran's leader has given the world every reason to believe, that if given the opportunity, he wouldn't hesitate to commit genocide. In his mind every problem in the world can be laid at Israel's doorstep. Israel's acting Prime Minister, Ehud Olmert, has accurately accused Iran's President of being *"obsessed with anti-Semitic hatred."*

Ahmadinejad is a Shiite Muslim who is deeply committed to an Islamic Messianic figure known as Mahdi (Arabic for "rightly-guided one") or sometimes referred to as the Hidden Imam... [25]

Anton La Guardia makes this chilling observation about Ahmadinejad's "Apocalypse Now" theology:

All streams of Islam believe in a divine saviour, known as the Mahdi, who will appear at the End of Days. A common rumour—denied by the government but widely believed---is that Mr. Ahmadinejad and his cabinet have signed a 'contract' pledging themselves to work for the return of the Mahdi and sent it to Jamkaran. Iran's dominant 'Twelver' sect believes this will be Mohammed ibn Hasan, regarded as the 12ᵗʰ Imam, or righteous descendant of the Prophet Mohammad. He is said to have gone into 'occlusion' in the ninth century, at the age of five. His return will be preceded by cosmic chaos, war and bloodshed. After a cataclysmic confrontation with evil and darkness, the Mahdi will lead the world to an era of universal peace. This is similar to the Christian version of the Apocalypse. Indeed, the Hidden Imam is expected to return in the company of Jesus. Mr. Ahmadinejad appears to believe that these events are close at hand and that ordinary mortals can influence the divine timetable. The prospect of such a man obtaining nuclear weapons is worrying. [26]

Within Shiite Islam, which dominates Iran, this 12th Imam is a spiritual leader who is of the bloodline of the prophet Muhammad.

According to Islamic teaching, he will return near the end of the world. According to their end-time view, when he returns, he will rule the earth for seven years, bringing about the Final Judgment and end of the world.

The mention of a seven-year rule for the Mahdi is interesting since the Bible predicts that the Antichrist or False Messiah will hold sway over the earth for seven years, ruling the entire world for the final half of the seven-year period.

MAHDI ARMY ATTACKS U.S. TROOPS

U.S. officials say they have found the smoking gun that confirms Iranian support for terrorists in Iraq: brand-new weapons fresh from Iranian factories. A senior U.S. defense official says coalition forces have recently seized Iranian-made weapons and munitions that bear manufacturing dates in 2006.

It appears, according to a U.S. defense official, that the material is going directly from Iranian factories to Shiite militias, rather than moving through black marketers. That clearly indicates that there is no way this is being done without the knowledge and support of the Iranian government. Iranian-made munitions found in Iraq include advanced IED's designed to pierce armor and anti-tank weapons. Iran's Islamic Revolutionary Guards Corps, which is believed to be training Iraqi militia fighters in Iran, is thought by U.S. intelligence to be supplying the weaponry to Iraq's growing Shiite militias.

Evidence is mounting that the most powerful militia in Iraq, Moktada al Sadr's Mahdi Army – now believed to be 40,000 strong – is receiving training support from the Iranian-backed terrorists of Hezbollah. Two senior U.S. defense officials confirmed to ABC News that fighters from the Mahdi army have traveled to Lebanon to receive training from Hezbollah. (ABC News, November 30, 2006) [27]

According to CBN News, "Whether it is his belief

that Israel should be wiped off the map, denials of the Holocaust, obsession with going nuclear, or support for radical Islamic terrorist groups, Mahmoud Ahmadinejad is a man on a divine mission. Behind the Jamkaran mosque, there is a well. According to many Shiite Muslims, out of this well will one day emerge their version of an Islamic savior. They call him the Mahdi, or the 12th Imam. Enter Mahmoud Ahmadinejad. Since becoming the president of Iran in August, 2005, Ahmadinejad has emerged as the Mahdi's most influential follower. He has stated that his mandate is to pave the way for the coming of this Islamic messiah. In almost all of his speeches, the president begs Allah to hasten the return of the Mahdi. Ahmadinejad is reportedly tied to a radical Islamic society in Iran that believes man can hasten the appearance of the Mahdi by creating chaos in the world. Ahmadinejad has stated that this chaos must take place before the Mahdi can come." [28]

According to a <u>NEWSWEEK</u> interview (August 21, 2006), one U.S. military intelligence official, requesting anonymity because of the sensitivity of the information, says of the rogue Iraqi elements, "The biggest threat now in Baghdad is the Mahdi Army." [29]

In a <u>WASHINGTON POST</u> article (August 24, 2006), Ellen Knickmeyer writes, "Pumping their fists in the air, the men and boys inside the colonnaded mosque shouted their loyalty to Shiite Muslim leader Moqtada al-Sadr. 'Hasten the coming of the Mahdi!' thousands chanted in the baking sun of the open-air mosque, summoning the central religious figure of Sadr's movement. 'And curse his enemies!' Sadr has become the most pivotal force in Iraq after the United States. The Sadr movement's ultimate goal is a 'united Islamic state,' Bahaa al-Araji, a senior lawmaker in the Sadr political bloc, said in an interview." [30]

In President Ahmadinejad's speech before the United Nations' General Assembly on September 19, 2006, he ended the speech with this, *"I emphatically declare that today's world, more than ever before, longs for just and righteous people with love for all humanity; and above all longs for the perfect righteous human being and the real savior who has been promised to all peoples and who will establish justice, peace and brotherhood on the planet. O, Almighty god, all men and women are your creatures and You have ordained their guidance and salvation. Bestow upon humanity that thirsts for justice, the perfect human being promised to all by You, and make us among his followers and among those who strive for his return and his cause."* [31]

According to the Hadith, the Koran and the Islamic end time teaching that's in their holy books, they believe that the Mahdi, this final restorer of justice, will return to the earth with Jesus. They believe that Jesus will boldly proclaim to the world that: *"I lied to you. I'm not actually divine. I'm not the Son of God…"* Islam teaches in their eschatology that Jesus will help convert all the Christians at the end of days to Islam.

It's not one individual that is coming. The Book of Revelation says that there are two. There's the beast, known as the man of sin; but then there's his partner we call the false prophet, who I boldly tell you will be an apostate pope, representing Christianity. The Islamic world is looking for their Mahdi. We know he will be the man of sin. He will be who we call the Antichrist. But here you have the president of Iran boldly preparing for his return.

The JERUSALEM POST documented this in January of this year, "He often raises the topic, and not just to Muslims. When addressing the United Nations in September, Ahmadinejad flummoxed his audience of world political leaders..." Here he is, standing in a United Nation's assembly, preaching and teaching to them, and giving his address, "...by concluding his address with a prayer for the Mahdi's appearance." At the end of his message he prays, "O mighty Lord," and of course that's Allah, "I pray to you to hasten the emergence of your last repository, the Promised One, that perfect and pure human being, the one that will fill this world with justice and peace."

By the way, this same individual denies the Holocaust. He says, "They have invented a myth that Jews were massacred and place this above God, religions and the prophets." He said, "The West claims that more than six million Jews were killed in World War II and to compensate for that they established and support Israel. If it is true that the Jews were killed in Europe, why should Israel be established in the East, in Palestine? Our question is, if you have committed this huge crime, why should the innocent nation of Palestine pay for this crime?"

Concerning threats to Israel, listen to what this same man said, "Anybody who recognizes Israel will burn in the fire of the Islamic nation's fury. Remove Israel before it is too late and save yourself from the fury of nations in the region. The skirmishes in the occupied land are part of a war of destiny. The outcome of hundreds of years of war will be defined in Palestinian land. As the Imam said, Israel must be wiped off the map. Israel is a tyrannical regime that will one day be destroyed. Israel is a rotten, dried tree that will be annihilated in one storm." [32]

I've got news for him. There is a God in Heaven that neither slumbers nor sleeps. And He, and He alone, is the protector of Israel! We are moving toward rapidly what is the final battle between all that is Godly, and all that is holy and all that God has said will come to pass, and every evil enemy that has opposed it for six thousand years. What is before us is the climax of all of history.

Muslim author, Harun Yahya, writes in his book, THE END TIMES AND THE MAHDI,

"Some important explanations about the End Times are as follows: During the terrible chaos of the final times, Allah will use a servant having superior morality known as the Mahdi (the guide to the truth), to invite humanity back to the right path. The Mahdi's first task will be to wage a war of ideas within the Islamic world and to turn those Muslims who have moved away from Islam's true essence back to true belief and morality. At this point, the Mahdi has three basic tasks:

1. Tearing down all philosophical systems that deny Allah's Existence and support atheism.
2. Fighting superstition by freeing Islam from the yoke of those hypocritical individuals who have corrupted it, and then revealing and implementing true Islamic morality based on the rules of the Qur'an.
3. Strengthening the entire Islamic world, both politically and socially, and then bringing about peace, security and well-being in addition to solving societal problems.

"According to many hadiths, Prophet 'Isa(Jesus) will return to Earth at the same time, and will call upon all Christians and Jews, in particular, to abandon their current superstitions and to live by the Qur'an. As the Christians hearken to him, the Islamic and Christian worlds will come together in one faith, and the world will experience that period of great peace, security, happiness, and well-being known as the Golden Age."

The noted Muslim author goes on to explain, "'There will be a dusty and smoky tribulation like patches of dark night...' (Abu Dawud). The word 'tribulation (fitnah)' implies anything that turns peoples' reason and hearts away from the true path, or war, incitement, chaos, disorder and conflict. The tribulation in the hadith will leave smoke and dust behind it, we learn."

"Furthermore, the way that tribulation is described as 'darkness' in the hadith, can be seen as an indication that its origins are unclear, that it is unexpected. Looking at it from that regard, it is probably that the hadith is referring to one of the world's worst terrorist attack, on the cities of New York and Washington in the United States on September 11, 2001."

"Therefore, this most saddening act of terror, which caused the live and injuries of thousands of innocent people, may well be that 'tribulation like patches of dark night' foretold by the hadith as the sign of the Mahdi's emergence." [33]

THE IRANIAN CONNECTION

The modern nation of Iran began in 1921 with a man named Reza Khan, who led the Cossack Brigade. On February 21, 1921, he brought his Cossack Division into Tehran and by 1923 he was installed as the new shah. He took the name Reza Shah Pahlavi. During his tenure, Reza Shah focused on modernization and industrialization. He was fascinated with the rise of Germany in the 1930's and considered the Persians a fellow Aryan state with Germany. The name changed from Persia (land of Persia) to Iran (land of the Aryans) in 1935. [34]

"Islam makes it incumbent on all adult males, provided they are not disabled and incapacitated, to prepare themselves for the conquest of other countries so that the writ of Islam is obeyed in every country of the world." – Ayatollah Khomeini (1948)

No one should think Iran's "Islamic revolution" is over. The Islamic republic's present rulers have not abandoned the world view of their founder, Grand Ayatollah Ruhollah Khomeini, who declared Saudi Arabia's rulers unfit to be the guardians of Islam's holiest cities, Mecca and Medina, and who first branded the United States as "the Great Satan."

Sanctions have not stopped Iran from exporting its Islamic revolution to Shi'ite-controlled Lebanon and sponsoring Hezbollah terrorism against Israel. And now the International Atomic Energy Agency is sounding the alarm about Iran's nuclear development.

Iran seems to be on the verge of becoming a nuclear power despite the best efforts of the U.S. and the world community to prevent it. The time for diplomacy is running out, while Iran's nuclear arms program approaches critical mass.

"When I read the recent (intelligence) reports regarding Iran, I saw a monster in the making," said Dr. Yuval Steinitz, chair of the Israeli Knesset's foreign and defense committee. He is concerned that Iran's ability to build a nuclear bomb may be as little as a year away. "There is only one option that is worse than military action," he said, "and that is to sit by and do nothing." [35]

CHAPTER 7

The Hashemite Dynasty

Let's take a moment and explain the importance of the Hashemite Dynasty. It is impossible to understand the fabric of the Middle East in modern history without having a working knowledge of this royal family. The Hashemites, or the "Bani Hashem", are descendents of the Arab chiefton Quraysh, who in Muslim tradition is believed to be a descendant of Ishmael, the son of Abraham. The name "Hashem" originated with the great-grandfather of the Prophet Muhammad.

The Hashemites are thus the direct descendants of Muhammad – this is extremely important - through his daughter Fatima and her husband Ali Bin Abi Talib, who was also Muhammad's paternal first cousin and the fourth caliph of Islam. The Hashemites ruled the holy city of Mecca until 1925, yet remain the acknowledged sovereign possessors of rite to all Islamic holy sites. That is critically important. Do not let that get by you. The Hashemites that ruled as descendants of Muhammad are the sovereign possessors of the rite to all Islamic holy sites. A Hashemite king carries a long established history within Islam as the "guardian of the Islamic faith and the Holy City of Jerusalem!"

To this day, the very site we Christians know as the Jewish Temple Mount, is known throughout Islam as

"Haram el Sharif", and overseen by the Jordanian group, the "Waqf"("Islamic Trust") by the rule of the Jordanian Hashemite Kingdom; in this case currently King Abdullah, and formerly Hashemite King Hussein of Jordan. If you've ever seen the golden-crowned Dome of the Rock, where the Temple once stood, that is Islam's third holiest site, that gold was paid for out of King Hussein's coffers.

Why? Because he was the prominent Hashemite king, again, as the custodians and _**guardians**_ of this Islamic holy site. Technically the nation we all call Jordan, is in reality known as "The Hashemite Kingdom of Jordan."

In 1916, Hussein ibn Ali, then head of the al Hashem clan, which again is the Hashemites, launched the Arab revolt against the Ottoman rule and proclaimed himself "King of all the Arab countries," though the allies only recognized him as ruler of the Hejaz, the western region of what is now Saudi Arabia. Long before there was a Saudi Arabia, that land was controlled by the Hashemites. This is where Saudi Arabia came from. He declared himself to be "The Caliph" in 1924, but was forced to abdicate after a Wahabi invasion, led by Abdul Aziz ibn Saud. In the 1920s – this is important – Hussein's sons, Faisal and Abdullah – he had two sons – they became rulers and kings of two nations: One was Iraq, and one was Transjordan. The Hashemite rule continues in Jordan.

It was passed down from King Hussein, who died in 1999, to his son Abdullah. However Iraq's Hashemite King Faisal was slain in 1958 by a coup led by Saddam Hussein and his insurgents. Today, could Iraq, known as ancient Babylon, biblically, be positioned for the emergence of another Hashemite leader to claim his role as king?

Let's get to Assyria, because I showed you earlier that the Antichrist will be called, known, designated, and identified as "The Assyrian." Ancient Assyria, when compared to our modern map, consisted of the nations now known as Syria, Jordan and Iraq. This region was also known as Transjordan until 1916. This same region of the Middle East was controlled for generations by the Royal Family of the Hashemites.

The Man of Sin **must** come from this particular and specific region of the Middle East. So why do prophetic students continue to look solely to Rome or Europe when attempting to identify the Antichrist? Anyone identified as "The Assyrian" must come from ancient Assyria. This Man of Sin will most definitely have ties and connections to Rome. He's leading a revived Roman Empire. (I would submit that the president of the Club of Rome would fit that. More on this in Chapter 8).

Even the ancient original Roman Empire consisted of far more than Rome, and far more than even the European region. It included major portions of the current Middle Eastern region, and nearly all of the current Arab Muslim controlled nations. It also includes huge portions of Arab Muslim land. This is a vital point, and it continues to be neglected by modern prophetic preaching.

Have we been looking in the wrong place when seeking to identify the Man of Sin?

Is the Hashemite rule really rising again?

I have a picture that was taken almost four years ago of the Gulf of Aqaba. A gigantic flag was constructed in Jordan at the port city of Aqaba. Its dimensions are enormous. The flag is over three football fields in size. Obviously, they wanted some people a long way away to see this. It's on a pole that's nearly five hundred feet high.

It's actually been identified as the royal flag of the Hashemite dynasty. Why would Jordan put up an enormous flag, three times the size of a football field, and put the flag of the ancient Hashemite dynasty up there, instead of the Jordanian flag?

I've searched a good Internet site (DEBKAfile.com) for the answer to that important question. They stated this:

"The Hashemites never gave up their claim of common descent from the Prophet Muhammad, or their vision of returning to their roots. This flag may be interpreted as a message that the Hashemite branch, which once ruled Baghdad, has not relinquished its claim there, either." [36]

They also say in the article that they're sending "a message" to Saudi Arabia. The ancient Islamic Hashemite Kingdom desires to control Baghdad again.

We know the Antichrist is going to peaceably take control of Saudi Arabia. There's only one family member that can pull that off, the man that can lay claim of his predecessors that once ruled that land. And he won't do it with a coup. This man's whole message is 'democracy', and, "You embrace me, and I'll embrace you. I won't force my way in," until he gets to the midpoint of the tribulation.

Who is this possible Man of Sin?

CHAPTER 8

Man Of Sin Possibly Identified?

God's Word has already given us the Man of Sin's identity! There are three significant titles given to us in the Scriptures of this man's identity.

1. The Assyrian.

"Therefore thus saith the Lord GOD of hosts, O my people that dwellest in Zion, be not afraid of __the Assyrian__: he shall smite thee with a rod, and shall lift up his staff against thee, after the manner of Egypt." – Isaiah 10:24

2. The Prince.

Daniel 9:26 makes it very clear that it is the prince that shall come and shall destroy the city and the sanctuary.

"And after threescore and two weeks shall Messiah be cut off, but not for himself: and the people of __the prince__ that shall come shall destroy the city and the sanctuary; and the end thereof shall be with a flood, and unto the end of the war desolations are determined." – Daniel 9:26

3. The King of Babylon.

The identity of the Man of Sin is given to us in Isaiah 14:4, and he is called the **king of Babylon**.

"That thou shalt take up this proverb against the __king of Babylon__, and say, How hath the oppressor ceased! the golden city ceased!" – Isaiah 14:4

The coming Man of Sin must carry all three of these titles!

A very interesting man already exists within the Muslim world. This man may be new to your personal knowledge, but he's not new to the world scene. In fact, after researching over the last four years for hundreds of countless hours, this one man; his ancestry, his honors, his influence, his words, his actions and his personal life mission, I have concluded that there is no other man like this man in the world today!

This man could possibly fit the Biblical pattern of the Man of Sin. But time will tell, and it's up to all other students of the prophetic Scriptures to judge for themselves whether this man does in fact meet the Biblical criteria.

The man's name is His Royal Highness Crown Prince El Hassan bin Talal. In the coming months and coming years, if I am correct, you're going to see more of this man.

No other man, among all other men, in the Islamic world, can claim his personal identity, to match all these distinctive signs than only one man:

His Royal Highness Crown Prince El Hassan bin Talal.

The Mahdi has to prove he's a descendent of Muhammad

through Fatima. There is only one family in the whole Islamic world that can do that. It is the Hashemite family. The Mahdi has got to be a Hashemite.

More modest and less flamboyant than his late brother, King Hussein, Prince Hassan is widely regarded as a man of dignity, knowledge and impeccable connections; a man with an intimate knowledge of cultural, religious and political issues of the Middle East. His ascension to power in Iraq (Yes, Iraq, not his native home of Jordan) would put a friend of the United States in power, help ease tensions with Israel and informally unite Jordan and Iraq, as a counterweight to regional rivals such as Syria, Iran and Saudi Arabia.

If you were to see a picture of Prince El Hassan, you would notice two distinct things. He has a broad, huge forehead. He has an unmistakably prominent, even somewhat pointed nose. This is important.

Let me tell you a little bit about this man.

His Royal Highness Crown Prince El Hassan bin Talal was born in Amman, Jordan, on March 20th, 1947. His Royal Highness is the younger brother of His Late Majesty King Hussein. Their branch of the Hashemite family is directly descended from the Prophet Muhammad, and is the forty-second generation. El Hassan, though a Muslim, actually graduated from Christ Church, Oxford University with a B.A. in Oriental Studies.

He is also the recipient of many honorary degrees, including the Honorary Degree of Doctor of Humane Letters, Spertus Institute of Jewish Studies; in addition he has an Honorary Doctorate of Theology from the faculty of Catholic Theology at Eberhard-Karls University in Tubingen, Germany.

I am writing today to let you know that there is a Muslim prince in the world who is a direct descendant of Muhammad, and is honored by Christian churches, Jewish synagogues and ministries, and Catholic theology!

On the international stage, many of Prince El Hassan's ideas and initiatives have acted as a catalyst for worldwide organizations. He addressed the 36th session of the United Nations in 1981. His Royal Highness proposed the establishment of the New International Humanitarian Order, which led to his being asked by the Secretary General to found and co-chair the Independent Commission on International Humanitarian Issues, or (ICIHI).

He was back in the news in a prominent way after the tragedy of the tsunami. He is going back to what he said in the U.N., and is saying much about that today – humanitarian efforts. Prince El Hassan also chairs and is a member of numerous international committees and organizations. I challenge you to go to the list and read it yourself.

He's a member of the International Board of the Council on Foreign Relations. He's a member of UNESCO World

Commission on Culture and Development. He's the President of the Board of Directors for the Center for Peace Studies and Conflict Resolution. He is also the **President** of the **Club of Rome**.

In the field of religion, His Royal Highness' contact and meetings have evolved into a systematic interfaith dialogue, primarily consisting of three ongoing consultations with the Orthodox Centre of the Ecumenical Patriarchate in Chambesy, Switzerland; the Pontifical Council for Inter-religious dialogue at the Vatican; and the Independent Commission on Christian-Muslim-Jewish relations through the ages of the Deanery of Windsor. Notice: Christian, Muslim and Jewish – this man's goal in life is to fix the problems and the rift between the Jews, the Muslims and the Christians.

His Royal Highness set up the Royal Institute for Inter-Faith Studies in 1994. In 1999, Prince El Hassan was a founding member and became Vice Chairman of the Foundation for Inter-Religious and Intercultural Research and Dialogue, located in Geneva, Switzerland.

In November of 1999 at the 7th World Assembly of the World Conference on Religion and Peace (WCRP), held in Amman, where he currently lives, Prince El Hassan accepted the position of "Moderator" of the World Conference on Religion and Peace.

El Hassan has authored numerous books, including: "A Study on Jerusalem," "Christianity in the Arab World," and "To Be A Muslim." I have them in my possession. I'm probably the only prophecy preacher in the world that not only has all three of these books, but also has read every word of them. He is fluent, by the way, in Arabic, English and French, and has a working knowledge of German, Spanish, and Turkish. This Muslim, descendant of Muhammad, studied Biblical Hebrew as part of his degree course. The man knows seven languages.

Incidentally, Israel became recognized as a state on May 14, 1948. We all use that date. However that's technically inaccurate. On that date is when America and other nations recognized it. The actual date of November 29th, 1947 was when the UN Partition Plan was adopted by the General Assembly, by international vote, of which Israel then later recognized her own State Declaration in 1948.

Israel's "birth" was technically linked to 1947. Oddly, yet perhaps prophetically, El Hassan himself was born in 1947!

Should it surprise us that as the God of Israel was at work in the earth, bringing BIRTH to His final nation, people and end time plan, that Satan also was possibly at work in the earth, giving BIRTH to his Man of Sin and his end time plan? Just "coincidence," I don't think so!

CLUB OF ROME

Prince El Hassan became the President of the Club of Rome. The Club of Rome is the number one think tank in the world, moving behind the scenes to bring the world into global government. He was appointed the President of the Club of Rome in Madrid on November 28th, 2000.

He said this: "We come together in the context of universal values. I personally question the coinage of 'globalism' and prefer the term 'universalism', because we share in universal values…I recognize the work of one of our distinguished colleagues in the Club of Rome, who refers continuously to one civilization with ten thousand cultures. We come together in the context of knowledge and of innovation and to speak of globalization as a fact which must be faced squarely. I call for an ethic of human understanding, for an ethic of human solidarity. I would like to suggest that in today's troubled world, the inter-religious reactions to events, in many parts of the world, not least of all my own, which have now assumed hegemonal, national dimensions."

The man is absolutely brilliant.

What is the Club of Rome? See for yourself at www.clubofrome.org.

In their own words, "The Club of Rome is a global think tank and centre of innovation and initiative. As a non-profit, non govermental organisation (NGO), it brings together scientists, economists, businessmen, international high civil servants, heads of state and former heads of state from all five continents who are convinced that the future of humankind is not determined once and for all and that each human being can contribute to the improvement of our societies."

The Club of Rome's mission is to act as a global catalyst of change that is free of any political, ideological or business interest.

The Club of Rome contributes to the solution of what it calls the world problematique, the complex set of the most crucial problems – political, social, economic, technological, environmental, psychological and cultural – facing humanity.

It does so taking a global, long term and interdisciplinary perspective aware of the increasing interdependence of nations and the globalization of problems that pose predicaments beyond the capacity of individual countries.

The Club of Rome's essential mission is to act as an independent, global, non-official catalyst of change. It aims at the following:

- The identification of the most crucial problems facing humanity, their analysis in the global context of the world-wide problematique, the research of future alternative solutions and the elaboration of scenarios for the future.
- The communication of such problems to the most important public and private decision-makers as well as to the general public.

The Club of Rome is governed by three complementary principles:

1. A global perspective in examining issues with the awareness that the increasing interdependence of nations and the globalization of problems pose predicaments beyond the capacity of individual countries.

2. Holistic thinking and the seeking of a deeper understanding of complexity within the contemporary problems – political, social, economic, technological, environmental, psychological and cultural – which the Club of Rome terms, the world problematique.

3. An interdisciplinary and long-term perspective focusing on the choices and policies determining the destiny of future generations, because this perspective is too often neglected by governments and other decision-makers on account of short-term interests. [37]

As well-meaning as these lofty goals and objectives are, many, many sectarian and theological scholars have great mis-givings about the Club of Rome, which is made up of 100 active members who are extremely, extremely influential. Many believe this Club represents the foundation of the One-World Government and New World Order. This semi-secretive organization was founded in 1968 as a European "think tank" and addresses various stressful issues to help solve them as they prepare for the coming New World Order.

Aurelio Peccei founded the Club of Rome and has called for a world dictator, "A charismatic leader – scientific, political, or religious – would be the world's only salvation from the social and economic upheavals that threaten to destroy civilization. Such a leader would have to override national and international interests as well as political and economic structures in order to lead humanity away from the maladies that afflict it...only a revolution, the substitution of a new world economic order can save us!" [38]

Need I write more. You can see where this group is heading.

Of course, its President is His Royal Highness Crown Prince El Hassan bin Talal of Jordan.

Prince El Hassan uses big words. In fact he invents new words. He takes words and brings them together: "hegemonal, national dimensions, need a cool head and a warm heart – not to judge others, not to challenge the legitimacy of fear, but to offer a beacon of hope. When meeting with my colleagues in the International Inter-religious Foundation of the U.K., I would like to assure you that as Jews, Christians and Muslims, if we observe on Friday, Saturday and Sunday strictly, we would never see each other. We then move to fear of the folks back home...I recognize with great warmth the importance of developing peace in this troubled world."

"I recognize in particular the words of a peacemaker of yesteryear, my colleague, Shimon Peres, who said not so long ago that to achieve peace, we need to achieve peace at home. And I say here we have to achieve peace with ourselves; we have to achieve peace with our neighbors; and we have to achieve and develop peace with the modern age. I hope we are not leaping into the future when we speak only of peace with modernity; I hope we can also speak of bringing the old world into the new age."

He concluded by saying this, "In this common human privilege, which we all share, there are no privacies and no monopolies, no exclusive holiness, no 'peculiar peoples;' only distinctive races, climates, living spaces and environments, and a rich diversity of cultures - all under God in an equal benediction and at a comparable risk to their 'ever generous Lord'."

"The 'excellence' of Jerusalem is to have been, and to remain, one (redoubtable) of such capital cities summoned, as such, to be the 'joy of the whole earth'." [39]

Why does he talk about Jerusalem being the joy of the whole earth? He boldly says that there are no "special monopolies" and no "exclusive holiness" and no "particular peculiar" peoples. He's got an agenda. He desires to "bring the old world" into "a new age!"

In his latest book, TO BE A MUSLIM: ISLAM, PEACE, AND DEMOCRACY, which came out post 9/11, El Hassan recognizes this new "clash of civilizations," the post 9/11 struggle between Islam and the West. El Hassan writes this current work to offer his personal answers and assurances that Islam means us supposedly "no harm!" According to this Crown Prince, Islam is a "peaceable and just religion."

This book spells out his goals, his agenda and his mission more completely than anything else he's written. It's "must reading" if one seeks to accurately and fully picture this unique man. The book's back cover says this: "This book is an incisive, personal statement about the essence of Islam by one of the world's leading advocates of inter-faith dialogue and understanding – Prince El Hassan bin Talal of Jordan."

There is much ignorance about Islam in the West, and negative opinions of Islam feed on that ignorance. The views and attitudes about Islam, and public dialogue since the Osama bin Laden-inspired terrorist attack on September 11, 2001, require a response, a response that sets Islam in a light that shows its fundamental belief structures and its humanity. The core of this book is a statement of belief, in a question and answer format that allows Islam's basic tenets to be quickly grasped by a wide audience. Prince El Hassan's answers are precise and informative.

The books promo continues, "He presents a persuasive argument that the beliefs and culture of the majority of the Islamic world not only are compatible with but are contributive to a world at peace – a world of diversity in which Muslim and non-Muslim nations can and should collaborate to create a more humane and just global society." [40]

He cites the Qur'an, the Hadith (sayings), and the Sunna (tradition) of the prophet Muhammad, and he describes how most of Islam during most of its history has applied the teachings of the Prophet so as to treat other ethnic groups, cultures and faiths – 'especially the Jewish and Christian monotheists' – with respect, tolerance and fairness.

In one post-9-11 speech, Prince El Hassan said, "Muslims, Christians and Jews have a common shared history…We are moving toward a single world with a single agenda and that agenda must be set with a view to fostering reconciliation and understanding." [41]

"We, the Children of Abraham, may claim to look in different directions for culture and custom, spirituality and succor, but this small patch of scorched, embattled earth cannot be divided by fences and false borders of the mind. If the political play does not allow us to admit this to those whose map of our region is distorted by self-interest and misguided strategic obstinacy, then at least let us have the sense to admit it to each other….

"In memory of my late brother, His Majesty King Hussein, and Yitzhak Rabin, we must strive not to wage wars, but to win peace. Real peace must be built; it is not just the absence of war. We need to talk about the end-game, to develop regional understanding, to address the energy issue that is at the heart of so much instability, and to devise a multilateral approach to such thorny issues as the proliferation of Weapons of Mass Destruction, together with a regional concept for human rights, prosperity and security." [42]

He told the <u>JERUSALEM POST</u> that a culture of respect for diversity should be emphasized in the education of both Israelis and Jordanians, "…since we are all stakeholders in a common future." [43]

Be sure to read all of his peacemaking and global efforts that truly put him on course as a possible man of sin. Visit his website at: www.elhassan.org.

Once again we're reminded of the words of Daniel the prophet, because he said, ***"but he shall come in peaceably, and he'll obtain the kingdom by flatteries…"***

"And in his estate shall stand up a vile person, to whom they shall not give the honour of the kingdom: but he shall come in peaceably, and obtain the kingdom by flatteries. – Daniel 11:21

CHAMPION OF THE EARTH

In a press release issued at United Nations' Headquarters in New York on Thursday, February 8, 2007, **"HRH Prince El Hassan Named UN Champion of the Earth.**

"The President of the Club of Rome, HRH Prince El Hassan bin Talal, is among the seven named by the United Nations Environment Programme (UNEP) as Champion of the Earth for his effort to save the world's environment.

"The 2007 laureates, from each of the world's regions, will be presented with their awards at a special ceremony in Singapore on 19 of April.

"Steering globalization onto a more intelligent and sustainable trajectory requires the commitment of Governments, the private sector, local authorities and civil society, but it also needs individuals capable of catalyzing change, empowering others and inspiring action," UNEP Executive Director Achim Steiner said.

"The men and women we are recognizing today are indeed role models who have committed themselves to realizing a more just, equitable and sustainable world" proof, if proof is needed, that globalization can be sustainably managed if we harness the intelligence, energy and vision so self evident in these Champions of the Earth 2007," he added. (www.clubofrome.org)

Think of it, the United Nations is already calling him a "Champion of the Earth!"

The Islamic Messiah, the Mahdi, uniquely qualifies to serve simultaneously as the Biblical Antichrist. We know that Islam explicitly denies the rightful role of Jesus the Christ.

"Beloved, believe not every spirit, but try the spirits whether they are of God: because many false prophets are gone out into the world. Hereby know ye the Spirit of God: Every spirit that confesseth that Jesus Christ is come in the flesh is of God: And every spirit that confesseth not that Jesus Christ is come in the flesh is not of God: and this is that spirit of antichrist, whereof ye have heard that it should come; and even now already is it in the world." – 1 John 4:1-3

We have already covered this a couple of chapters ago, but I want to reiterate the three essential Scriptural tests that someone must meet to indeed be "The Man of Sin:"

1. He must be Assyrian. Isaiah 10:24 points this out.
    "Therefore thus saith the Lord GOD of hosts, O my people that dwellest in Zion, be not afraid of the Assyrian: he shall smite thee with a rod, and shall lift up his staff against thee, after the manner of Egypt."

2. He must be a Prince. Daniel 9:26 refers to him as "the prince who is to come."
    "And after threescore and two weeks shall Messiah be cut off, but not for himself: and the people of the prince that shall come shall destroy the city and the sanctuary; and the end thereof shall be with a flood, and unto the end of the war desolations are determined."

3. He must be the King of Babylon, as confirmed in Isaiah 14:4.
    "That thou shalt take up this proverb against the king of Babylon, and say, How hath the oppressor ceased! the golden city ceased!"

Hear me loud and clear, I am NOT saying that this is the Man of Sin, but quite possibly this **COULD BE** the Man of Sin. There is one man in the world today that meets all of these criteria. He is His Royal Highness Prince El Hassan of the Hashemite Kingdom of Jordan.

Let's look how Prince El Hassan fulfills these requirements:

1. HE MUST BE ASSYRIAN.

Prince Hassan is genetically "Syrian". Dr. Elias of the California School of Medicine states, *"The closest genetic relationships of the Assyrians are with the native populations of Jordan and Iraq."*

Prince Hassan is allied with the Assyrian cause. The official website of the Assyrian Liberation Party hails the Prince as "an eloquent supporter of our position…for an Assyrian Province." Many Assyrians are Christian and, as such, are persecuted by their Islamic ethnic cousins. The Prince's support of the Assyrian cause would of course lend credence to the claim of him coming as a "man of peace."

Prince Hassan has royal connections to ancient Assyria. The Hashemite family has ruled extensively in the region; including Arabia, Jordan (currently) and Iraq. He has already been put forward as a candidate to resume the throne in Iraq both by his own doing, as well as by some Western interests.

2. HE MUST BE A "PRINCE"

Daniel 9:26 describes the Antichrist as the *"prince who is to come."* Prince El Hassan was the Crown Prince of the

Hashemite Kingdom of Jordan until just before the death of his brother, King Hussein. In a letter written just before his death, the King removed him, but wrote cryptically of a worldwide venue that would be his. He does, however, remain a Prince in Jordan.

3. HE MUST BE KING OF BABYLON

Referring to the time of the end, when God "will set them in their own land." Isaiah refers to this all-powerful Antichrist figure as "The king of Babylon." (Isaiah 14:14)

Babylon is located in modern day Iraq, located about 50 miles south of Baghdad. The city was part of a revival project begun by Saddam Hussein as a monument to his own power. Prince El Hassan is, as I will demonstrate in the next chapter, actively lobbying for the royal throne of Iraq. The Hashemite family has not relinquished its royal claim to Baghdad.

One final point has got to be made, as we go back again to the Book of Daniel. During the tribulation period, the Man of Sin will enter into the land of Israel, he'll claim royal rights to the Temple Mount in Jerusalem, and he'll commit the "abomination of desolation." In his height of military strength, he somehow fails to conquer and will not overcome one significant nation and people. Daniel 11:41 says: *"He shall also enter into the glorious land."* That's Israel. That's the midpoint of the tribulation. *"And many countries shall be overthrown: but these shall escape out of his hand, even Edom, and Moab, and the chief of the children Ammon."*

Somebody does not get slaughtered by him. Edom, Moab and the chief of the children of Ammon can only be identified as ONE MODERN NATION - and that is…**Jordan**. Let's use the proper, appropriate name -- The Hashemite Kingdom of Jordan!

Follow the picture now.

He's going to leave Babylon and go into Israel. He's got to go right through Jordan to get there. But yet Jordan is going to "escape out of his hand." This one important verse of scripture never has made sense <u>until now</u>.

The Man of Sin allows this nation to escape, perhaps because of "Family Ties". Prince El Hassan, who may soon become King El Hassan, King of Iraq (Babylon), will most certainly allow his nephew and fellow Hashemite ruler to remain safe and secure when he lays claim to the land of Israel.

This small prophetic point finally makes sense, perhaps for the first time. How can the Antichrist let Jordan escape? Possibly because he's the Crown Prince of Jordan. His nephew now is the king. He was supposed to become the king of Jordan. But he didn't get it, so he's looking for a new crown. He's looking for a new throne, one that fits the Bible, because he's not supposed to be the king of Jordan. He's supposed to be the king of Babylon. He's going to let his nephew Abdullah and Jordan escape.

In Isaiah 14:22, it says: *"For I will rise up against them, saith the LORD of Hosts, and cut off from Babylon the name, and remnant, and son, and <u>nephew</u>, saith the LORD."* It's the same passage that identifies the Antichrist as the *"king of Babylon."* Isaiah 14:4 names and identifies the coming Man of Sin as the king of Babylon.

Later on it describes the destruction that God pours out on this king, and mentions a nephew.

Who is this nephew?

Could this nephew to this Man of Sin be King Abdullah, fellow Hashemite King to El Hassan? Perhaps this may be also the meaning behind Isaiah's further prophecy given in chapter 14. After identifying the coming Antichrist as the king of Babylon, he describes God's judgment which will come upon this man who is ultimately indwelt by Satan, Lucifer himself, and makes mention of another person with him.

This "man of sin" has a "nephew" when he's judged by God, who receives judgment with him.

CHAPTER 9

A Crown Prince On The World Scene ...TODAY!

During the days leading up to the actual attack and war upon Suddam Hussein's rule of Iraq, many months of discussion, planning, and formulation occurred behind the scenes, between exiled Iraqi leaders and key nationalists from many nations. These very meetings were given coverage by the international press. As these meetings progressed around the world – now get in mind this is before we went in to attack Iraq and remove Saddam – As these meetings progressed around the world, from city to city, gathering to gathering, one man seemingly made invaluable input and leadership throughout this process.

Here's a news article from the <u>DAILY STAR</u>. It's an article entitled: *"Is it Prince Hassan's Moment?"*

"Can a Jordanian prince help Iraq along the path of democracy? ...Jordan's Prince Hassan, the brother of late King Hussein, says he hopes to go to Baghdad soon to attend a conference aimed at easing tensions between Iraq's feuding Shiite and Sunni Muslim communities..." He's going to fix the feuding Shiite and Sunnis: "Hassan thinks he can play a unifying role...The Prince said he has discussed his visit with members of some of Iraq's big tribes.

"He says, 'I found that in these meetings, I was able to be recognized as someone with a proven track record and not a newcomer to the scene.'" Oh he's not a newcomer. They all worship his great-great-great-great-great-great-great-great- forty-two times-grandfather. "If we could have a figurehead acceptable to all parties, that would be ideal,' one British official said." [44]

Let's look at another article. This is from Michael Rubin, an article entitled: *If Iraqis Want a King, Hassan of Jordan Could Be Their Man*. He said this: "Last weekend, more than seventy exiled Iraqi military officials and Ahmed Chalibi, met in London to discuss the ousting of Saddam Hussein." Again, this is all prior to the war in Iraq. "American diplomats, Pentagon officials and members of Vice President Dick Cheney's staff joined British colleagues. The surprise participant was Jordan's Prince Hassan bin Talal. Crown Prince for more than three decades, Hassan frequently served as regent while his brother, King Hussein, traveled abroad.

As Hussein was, Hassan is known for his moderation, his genuine desire for peace, his humor and his learning… Should he be interested, Hassan's experience and lineage… Hashemites claim direct descent from the Prophet Mohammad - give him the unique ability to usher a post-Saddam Iraq back into the family of nations, with him chairing a future constitutional convention and overseeing the reconciliation process. With Saddam's days numbered, Hassan's appearance in London may signal that Iraqis will have a future far brighter than their past." [45]

Professor Abdulaziz Sachedina writes in the <u>Jewish World News</u> in December 23, 2004, "It was Imam Ali, the Prophet Muhammad's son-in-law and the inspiration of Shiite Islam, who emphasized the importance of forgiveness and compassion to those in positions of power. It is true that throughout their history in Iraq the Shiites have suffered when the minority Sunnis controlled absolute power. And under Saddam Hussein, powerful Sunni officials committed terrible atrocities against the Shiites. Not long ago, after the war began in earnest in March, 2003, in a meeting with Iraqi religious leaders in Amman, I heard a prominent Iraqi Sunni leader, Professor-Shaykh Qubaisi, urge Prince Hassan of Jordan to take over Iraq, so that the Sunni influence would continue in this 'Arab' nation. The call appeared to suggest that if the Shiite majority were to come to power the 'Arab' character of Iraq would be lost." [46]

Another article appeared in the <u>FORWARD NEWS</u>, entitled: ***"Jordan Prince Said to Seek Iraqi Throne."*** You can go on the Internet and find countless articles about Crown Prince El Hassan. This is about a meeting in Paris, "Former Crown Prince Hassan of Jordan is not on the guest list of a high-level meeting between the main Iraqi opposition groups and American officials…Nevertheless he's bound to loom large as participants grapple with the all important question of who runs a post-Saddam Baghdad. Rumors are rife that the fifty-five-year-old Hassan is angling to become King of Iraq.

Although he claims he had come to London merely to

express solidarity, Hassan's name has been bandied around for a series of United Nations postings since he was pushed aside from the Jordanian throne, fueling speculation that he was looking for a job, if not a crown...An American expert on Iraq said some people might be thinking that a Hashemite ruler might be a good compromise between the Shiite and the Sunni Muslim factions because the Hashemite Family is believed to be descended from both Prophet Muhammad and his son-in-law Ali, the latter a seminal figure in the Shiite faith..." [47]

"Some point to the close relationship between Hassan and Ahmed Chalibi. Ahmed Chalibi was indicted in Jordan for bank fraud in the 1980s, and Hassan helped him get out of jail. In fact, Chalibi invited Hassan to London, several sources said." [48]

This is from the <u>ECONOMIST</u>, and it's entitled: *"A King for Iraq?"* The column says this:

"One of the more lively moments in last week's get-together of a group of Iraqi dissidents was when Prince Hassan, Jordan's elder statesman, strode into their London meeting place. He then embraced a [figure] of King Faisal, his murdered cousin and the last king of Iraq. And in conversation, Jordan's Hashemite prince spoke of 'assuming his ancestral responsibilities' in the region, harking back to the first world war, when his great-grandfather was the British appointed king of the Arabs, and his great-uncle was the king of Iraq." [49]

<u>C NEWS</u> gave this article entitled: *"Jordan's Prince Hassan Raises Concern – He's looking for a kingdom - in Iraq."*

Amman: "Prince Hassan's hopes of visiting Iraq in the near future is sparking fresh speculation that the onetime heir to the Jordanian throne is a prince in search of a kingdom…Hassan told Al-Arabiya satellite channel that he plans to visit Baghdad 'soon' to try to mediate political disputes… 'to try to facilitate negotiations among the different sects,' meaning the Sunni and the Shiites, and of course the Kurds. "An Iraqi political activist said the prince has been meeting in Jordan with some Iraqi tribal and religious leaders, trying to persuade them to support his involvement in resolving Iraq's political conflict. 'He does not tell them openly that he aspires to a leading role, like being king of Iraq, but this is what everybody feels when they meet him,' said the activist who spoke with the A.P. on condition of anonymity." [50]

El Hassan seems to aspire to a rulership role in the newly formed Iraqi government. Some will ask, "Well where is Prince El Hassan now? He wasn't elected as their new leader in Iraq." Yet, I can document how El Hassan has actually been the "invisible hand" each step of the way behind the scenes, personally overseeing and influencing the key players, and has helped design and define the very process of these elections in Iraq.

He is merely waiting until the opportune moment, and trusting those he has empowered now to empower him later. Hassan knows full well that these people cannot be forced or coerced, now that the decades under Saddam Hussein are over. He is seeking to come to power through "democratic" means and processes. That's very important. Not only that, it's unsafe to be in charge of anything in Iraq these days. He's waiting for the time when the violence is less intense to make his move.

Let's look at more interesting news reports however, concerning this point, in the "post-Saddam" time frame. One was actually covered by Al-Jazeereh. It originated in JORDAN TIMES. It was an article entitled, *"Iraqi Religious Leaders Call for Immediate Interim Government."* Here's what it says:

"Iraqi religious leaders on Wednesday wrapped up a two-day conference here, calling for an immediate interim government and free and direct elections…the gathering, organized by the New York based World Conference on Religion and Peace (WCRP)." [51]

Where have we seen this organization before?

"His Royal Highness Prince Hassan, who hosted the conference in his palace, highlighted the importance of the message of hope that religious leaders can convey to the Iraqi people in these troubled times… 'Saving lives and upholding the dignity of the Iraqi people is our sole aim in coming together,' Prince Hassan said. 'Pledging common action to assure a just society in Iraq.' El Hassan said, 'These religious leaders demonstrate that religion can be a powerful force for peace and for affirming our common humanity.'...The religious leaders gathered at the conference unanimously elected Prince Hassan to represent them in all regional and international venues regarding their shared commitment to collaborate on full reconstruction of Iraq." [52]

Is it time for "the prince" to become "king" within Iraq (Babylon)?

A FUTURE KING OF IRAQ?

"For he shall come up and shall become strong with a small people." – Daniel11:23

Brian Whitaker reported, in an article in THE GUARDIAN UNLIMITED (United Kingdom) entitled, *"A Prince Coming to the Aid of Babylon (Iraq)."*

"It was on July 12, 2002 at Kensington town hall in London exiled Iraqi army officers and opposition leaders were just about to start their much heralded talks on the overthrow of Saddam Hussein, when a cry of 'Media! Media!' summoned journalists to the back of the hall.

"As the double doors swung open, there in the glare of camera lights, stood Prince El Hassan bin Talal of the Hashemite Kingdom of Jordan." [53]

What on earth was he doing here? The article reports that it was a clearly a gesture of solidarity with the Iraqi opposition, but why again the news article questions. As the Prince made his stately way to the front, he took a seat next to Sharfi Ali bin Al-Hussein, a cousin of the last Iraqi King.

The meeting was then delayed for several minutes as Prince Hassan beamed at a dozen or more microphones thrust towards his face, but said nothing illuminating. He was attending merely as "an observer," though he later declared his support for "the Iraqis right to live in democracy, security and peace."

The report goes on to say, "The next day Jordan information minister, Mohammed Adwan, issued a statement denying that the Jordanian government had any prior knowledge of the Prince's attendance at the meeting, "which does not conform to the principled Jordanian stand on brotherly Iraq."

The article went on to write that constitutionally speaking the prince is a private citizen and can do what he likes. [54]

The August 22, 2002 meeting of top Iraqi officers would have gone less noticed were it not for the unexpected appearance of Prince Hassan bin Talal of Jordan, the late King Hussein's brother and the uncle of the Jordanian monarch, King Abdallah. In the words of one newspaper, Hassan "stole the show when he entered, ringed by TV cameras." Another paper characterized his presence at the conference as "the large vocal bomb". An Iraqi newspaper issued in London considered Hassan's appearance as subject to many interpretations not least of which was advancing "special interest of those present, as well as those of the United States which stands behind them."

Prince Hassan was the highest-ranking Arab official attending the officers' meeting. In his remarks Hassan insisted that his presence must be viewed as that of "an observer" with extensive friendships and family relationships with those present "including our cousin Al-Sharif Ali bin al-Hussein," who is the leader of the constitutional monarchy "enriching the struggle" against Saddam's regime particularly by the Arabs and Kurds. He went on to emphasize that, "We belong to the Shi'ites… and they belong to us." He then told the army officers: "The security we seek is not the security of the rifle, but as Allah has said, 'Feed them from hunger and secure them from fear.' In short, the prince appealed to all significant segments of Iraqi society the army officers, mostly Sunnis, the majority of Shi'ites who dominate southern Iraq and the Kurds who dominate the north of the country (the two regions where most of the huge Iraqi reservoir of oil and natural gas are found).

THE PARALLEL WITH AFGHANISTAN

Prince Hassan's appearance before the Iraqi officers perhaps goes beyond an expression of Jordanian displeasure toward Iraq's growing economic and commercial dealing with Syria and the Gulf countries. Prince Hassan may aspire to see the restoration of the Hasemites to Iraq, and his aspiration may not be entirely unrealistic. After all writes Mahdi Mustapha, "Who could have imagined that the exiled Afghanis in the West would return to govern Afghanistan after 40 years? Who has heard of Zaher Shah and Hamid Karzai, and why can't this be replicated in Iraq?" In a recent debate on the Qatari, Al-Jazeera television channel, the question of Hassan, serving as the karzai of Iraq was mentioned but not enriched by a serious debate.

PRINCE HASSAN MAKING WORLD HEADLINES AS POSSIBLE KING OF IRAQ

Others take note of Prince Hassan's involvement in Iraq. *"A time for Kings? Hashemites and others in the Arab mix,"* a report given by David Pryce-Jones from the September 2, 2002 issue of the NATIONAL REVIEW.

"Recently Hassan caused a sensation by turning up without warning at the conference in London of Iraqi opposition leaders, many of them ex-generals. Discreetly he claimed to be presenting merely as an observer, but he could not have made it plainer that if the position were open after the downfall of Saddam, he would be available to be 'King' of Iraq." [55]

"The man who could be King," Guardian Unlimited reports…

He should have been crowned King of Jordan but his brother had a deathbed change of heart. Now Prince

Hassan says he would happily mediate between Saddam Hussein and the world. Michael Freeland visited Prince Hassan at his home in Jordan.

Mr. Freeland started off the article by posing a question. "Could the man once destined to be King of Jordan end up as King of Iraq? Not if he has his way." Mr. Freeland writes. "Although the idea is being touted around the Middle East. But the former Crown Prince Hassan would not reject another notion being mooted that he should go to Baghdad as a mediator." [56]

Prince Hassan also stated in the article that "He is not wedded to the concept of either authoritarian monarchy or totalitarian republic," he says. "To be true to myself, I am wedded to the concept of recognizing we, the people, of this part of the world. I have no positional aspirations. I think it's for the people of Iraq to decide."

The article goes on to say that Prince Hassan is regarded as perhaps the world's most intelligent royal. He regularly flits from country to country, busy in his roles in a half-dozen non-governmental organizations.

Prince Hassan stated in the interview that he is not looking for a job but if asked to mediate between Saddam Hussein and the allies he would accept with alacrity, although he believes that the war is already won, "I would ask how do we win the peace?"

The trouble, he says, is that President Saddam has an

enormous "ego." He met the leader in 1990 when the Prince was cut off mid-question by an aide nine years earlier, he has met him to discuss the Iran-Iraq war and "disagrees with him fundamentally." But Hassan said he would give the mediation job a go, even though "I walk around with so many daggers in my back. I would say to Baghdad, remember that importance of plurality. I don't have an agenda, but I am prepared to go." [57]

The December 1, 2004 the <u>DAILY STAR</u> Reports: ***Is it Prince Hassan's moment?*** Reporter David Ignatius writes the following article.

"Jordan's Prince Hassan the brother of the late King Hussein, says he hopes to go to Baghdad soon to attend a conference aimed at easing tensions between Iraq's feuding Shi'ites and Sunni Muslim communities. As a Hashemite, Hassan thinks he can play a unifying role." [58]

From the BBC News Report April 15, 2003, *"Who's who in post Saddam Iraq,"*

A look at key figures who could lead the way, the report writes, Prince Hassan of Jordan is seen as an outside candidate among the royalists and is related to two former kings of Iraq, King Faisal I and King Faisal II. He is pressing for a role as an ambassador to Iraq. [59]

April 6, 2003 from the <u>Khalees Times</u> Online, *"Prince Hassan ready to play a role in Iraq."*

Jordan's Prince Hassan bin Talal, uncle of King Abdullah, said he is ready to play a role in coordinating the political reconstruction of post war Iraq.

He also rejected any U.S. administration, even temporary, in Baghdad.

Prince Hassan also stated that the period of transition and national reconciliation will be important and *"If I were called upon I would be willing to help with such a task as coordinator."* [60]

From <u>enews World</u> Jamal Halaby writes, "Jordan's Prince Hassan's hope of visiting Iraq in the near future is sparking fresh speculation that the one time heir to the Jordanian throne is a Prince in search of a Kingdom."

The report goes on to say, "Last week Hassan told Al-Arabiya satellite channel that he plans a visit to Baghdad 'soon' to try to mediate political disputes between factions in the country. He did not say with whom he would meet. The aide, speaking on condition of anonymity, said Hassan is waiting to be invited.

"When asked what Hassan would do in Iraq, the aide said he would try to facilitate negotiations and he will try to mediate between the Sunnis and the Shi'ites to restore peace and stability in Iraq" [61]

"If Iraqis want a King, Hassan could be their man," by Michael Rubin (2002):

"Last weekend, more than 70 exiled Iraqi military officials and Ahmad Chaibi, the head of the Iraqi National Congress, met in London to discuss the ousting of Saddam Hussein. American diplomats, Pentagon officials and members of Vice President Dick Cheney's staff joined British colleagues.

"The surprise participant was Jordan's Prince Hassan bin Talal, Crown Prince for more than three decades; Hassan frequently served as regent while his brother, King Hussein, traveled abroad. As Hussein was, Hassan is known for his moderation, his genuine desire for peace, his humor, and his learning.

"In his speech to the exiled Iraqi officers, Hassan avoided politics and focused instead upon his family's relationship with Iraq. His cousins ruled the country until 1958. He insisted his visit was strictly personal, telling reporters, 'I'm not carrying any signals.' Nevertheless, his address raises intriguing possibilities for Iraq's future." [62]

The next Recommendation comes from FOREIGN AFFAIRS: *"How to build a democratic Iraq"* by Adeed I. Dawisha and Karen Dawisha. May/June 2003,

Adeed I. Dawisha is professor of Political Science at Miami University, Ohio His latest book is "Arab Nationalism in the Twentieth Century: From triumph to Miami University, Ohio." Her books include the four volumes, Democratization and Authoritarianism in Post Communist Societies.

We would note this is the exact report that Prince Hassan directly mentions by name, in an interview with CNN's Mr. Wolf Blizter in June of 2004. Also he makes mention of this work at an award ceremony held in his honor the Rabbi Marc H. Tanenbaum Memorial lecture. Prince Hassan stated that Adeed Dawisha and Karen Dawisha have done a marvelous job of expressing everything he feels about Iraq.

Part of the report reads, "Splitting the executive between a weak president and a prime minister has a better chance of a sustaining democracy in Iraq. This division would allow political dueling to take place within the democratic tent, and not in the Iraqi street. A Prime Minster chosen by, and dependent on maintaining, a majority in the lower house of a bicameral parliament would serve as an institutional buttress against presidential abuse and would keep the affairs of the state running. Meanwhile, a charismatic president, chosen by the upper house, itself composed of the elected representatives of the 18 federal units, as well as notables and professionals, would function as the symbolic figurehead of the Iraqis.

"Another option that might work well for Iraq is restoring the Hashemite monarchy under strict constitutional limits. Because the Hashemites share the faith of Iraq's elite Sunni minority, restoration would reassure the Sunnis that the inevitable change in the balance of power will not lead to their marginalization. The monarchy also has the advantage of being well connected with tradition, which makes it a stabilizing force during a time of uncertainty and a barrier against extremism. A constitutional monarchy could become the symbol of Iraq's unity and civility and acts as the custodian of its positive traditional values. A monarchy would also help reassure Saudi Arabia and the other Persian Gulf states that they would no longer face the kind of threat Republican Iraq has long posed.

"Two obvious candidates for the throne would be Sherif Ali bin al-Hussein of Iraq or Prince Hassan bin Talal of Jordan. Both are cousins of Iraq's last king, Faisal II. Sherif Ali, a British-trained economist, is the current head of the Constitutional Monarchy Movement, an Iraqi opposition group. Prince Hassan, a graduate of Oxford University and the younger brother of Jordan's late King Hussein, has been a long time proponent of greater democracy in the Arab world." [63]

We need to pay very close attention to this last recommendation. This is from probably the premier scholar of Islam in the world. His name is Bernard Lewis, along with former CIA Director, James Woolsey, from the Clinton administration. Lewis and Woolsey penned an article in the WALL STREET JOURNAL entitled, *"After the War: King and Country, The Hashemite solution for Iraq,"* October 29, 2003. The article reads as follows:

"Conveniently, the 1925 constitution provides that the people of Iraq are deemed to have 'confided... a trust to King Faisal, son of Hussain, and to his heirs ...'. If the allies who liberated Iraq recognized an heir of this Hashemite line as its constitutional monarch, and this monarch agreed to help bring about a modern democracy under the rule of law, such a structure could well be the framework for a much smoother transition to democracy than now seems at hand. The Sunni Hashemites, being able to clam direct descent for the Prophet Mohammed, have historically been respected by the Shiites, who constitute a majority of the people of Iraq, although the latter recognize a different branch of the family. It is the Wahhabis of Saudi Arabia, not the Hashemites, who have been the Shiites' persecutors.

"The respect enjoyed by the Hashemites has been earned. They have had a generally deserved reputation for tolerance and coexistence with other faiths and other branches of Islam. Many Iraqis look back on the era of Hashemite rule from the 1920s to the 1950's as a golden age. And during the period of over 1,000 years when the Hashemites ruled the Hejaz, wherein the Muslim holy cities of Mecca and Medina are located; they dealt tolerantly with all Muslims during the Haj, or annual pilgrimage. Disagreement and tension under Hashemite rule have never come closer either to the bloody conflicts of many centuries' duration in Europe between Catholics and Protestants or to the massacres and hatred perpetrated by the Wahhabis and their allies in the House of Saud.

"During a transition in which Iraq is moving toward democracy, a government that is operating under its existing constitution, with a monarch as called for that document, is at least as legitimate as the governments of U.N. members that are not democracies at all. Much would hinge on the willingness of the king to work closely and cooperatively with Ambassador Bremer and to appoint a responsible and able Prime Minister. The king should be a Hashemite prince with political experience and no political obligations or commitments. In view of the nation's Shiite majority, the prime Minster should be a modern Shiite with a record of opposition to tyranny and oppression. Such leaders would be well-suited to begin the process that would in time lead to genuinely free and fair elections, sound amendments to the 1925 Iraqi Constitution and the election of a truly representative governing body. We would also strongly suggest that the choices of king and prime minister be made on the basis of character, ability and political experience, not on the basis of bias, self-interest, grudges or rivalries held or felt by some in the region and indeed by some in the U.S. government." [64]

Their choice for king of Iraq:
Prince El Hassan bin Talal.
The Hashemite solution.

CHAPTER 10

A Centrist Platform For Peace And Unity

Crown Prince El Hassan was the key partner with his older brother King Hussein, as Jordan negotiated the historic Peace Agreement with Israel. El Hassan, as "Crown Prince," was the heir to the throne, by the way. However, as King Hussein laid on his death bed, he made a mysterious change of heart and mind, and days before his actual death, he removed this title from his brother, and royally decreed it on his eldest son. Prince Abdullah, who is El Hassan's nephew, became the new heir to the throne as the King of Jordan. This sudden action led to great confusion and questions among the Arab world at that time.

In fact, there's a letter written by the Late Majesty King Hussein to his younger brother, his Royal Highness Prince El Hassan, January 25th, 1999. In that letter he gives this interesting closing excerpt, and I quote King Hussein's words to his brother:

"I thank you, your Royal Highness, my dear brother, and express my deepest appreciation to you for all the sincere efforts that you have exerted during the past three decades. This reflects what should ever be the case within our Hashemite Family and what should always be a pillar of the Hashemite Family of love and affection, a family which embodies a feeling of responsibility and understanding towards new developments and circumstances of a new era and regards these developments with a great deal of awareness and the ability to deal with them objectively and with selflessness.

I am sure that you are receiving this decision of mine with self-content, and with the spirit of a member of the one united Hashemite team. Jordan and the world at large will be your world, in which there are so many of issues in many fields that need your knowledge, expertise and deep intellect. " [65]

Why would he remove his brother from the throne in one breath, only to tell him in his next that the "whole world" will be his world? What are these "Hashemite responsibilities" that he must be loyal to in the circumstances of a "new era?"

A separate journalist named Helio Fred Garcia attended a prestigious gathering and wrote these telling remarks for his article in UN-World, dated May/June, 2004 in an article entitled *"Harnessing Religions in Pursuit of Peace."*

He wrote this, "On May 27th and 28th, 2003, in Amman, Jordan, Religions for Peace hosted a historic summit of all of Iraq's religious communities. The summit was hosted by Prince Hassan, and it was the first time since Saddam Hussein took power in 1979 that the Iraqi Sunni and Shiite communities met in the same room."

That's powerful – the first time in three decades that we get the leaders of these two groups together, and it's at El Hassan's palace.

"Dozens of religious leaders from around the world also attended, as observers and in solidarity, with their Iraqi brethren…For two days the delegates met in public session, and in private meetings, and over dinner with Prince Hassan.

"To me it resembled a combination of the United Nations Security Counsel meeting, complete with headphones for simultaneous translation, and a Chicago ward heeler getting a deal done with local politicians."

Do you see what he's saying there?

He's saying from one standpoint it looked like this U.N. gathering of all these dignitaries; but then another side of it was like one of those Chicago hucksters getting his political agenda pushed through. And he said this: "I also saw the hard-nosed with the holy. It's one thing to want peace, and it's quite another to make it happen.

"But I saw Prince Hassan work the delegates collectively, in groups and one-on-one, forehead-to-forehead." He even mentions the man's forehead. I was floored when he did that. He continues, "Prince Hassan met with them, one-on-one, forehead-to-forehead, to ensure that what was agreed to in Amman would work on the ground in Najaf and in Baghdad and in Mosul." [66]

Are you getting the picture? There is one unique man who can fix these problems.

Students of Bible prophecy have looked for a coming leader who supposedly is going to sign a peace treaty with Israel for seven years. This would then trigger the tribulation period. Good men have preached it, including me. It's not an untruth. It's just only a part of the truth. Let me explain.

The text actually uses the word "confirm." Now this word in the original language means, "to strengthen," and it implies that a covenant of peace – get this – this is important – a covenant of peace must exist already. It must exist previously, and then it will actually be "made possible" or "empowered" or "strengthened." He doesn't just show up one day and sign something. He comes and confirms or strengthens what's already there.

Is it possible then that this "covenant" already exists?

Quite possibly it is in the form of the current Oslo Accords, which was previously known as the "Treaty of Peace between the State of Israel and the Hashemite Kingdom of Jordan." This treaty was signed in October of 1994. You may recall seeing the pictures of this on television, the participants that sat there that signed that Peace Treaty. Sitting right there, next to President Bill Clinton and the rest of them, is the man that wrote it, Prince El Hassan.

The fact is Crown Prince El Hassan was the main originator, author, and intellect behind all the proceedings, behind all the formations and meetings, which culminated in this written and signed Peace Agreement between Israel and Jordan.

While prophecy students are waiting for some coming Man of Sin, who's supposedly going to sign this seven-year peace treaty… Is it possible that the actual Peace Treaty already exists, and it already bears the Man of Sin's signature?

Is it possible, that once in position as king of Iraq (Babylon), El Hassan will do exactly what the prophet Daniel said? He will finally be able to muster the might it will take to "confirm" what he's already got, and STRENGTHEN this covenant?

When Prince El Hassan finally "strengthens" this peace process, by the way, (which he's given his entire adult life to build), does he personally have a <u>time frame</u> in mind for this process? Wouldn't you agree that if we could pin him down on a time frame, that it would at least be significant? Let's ask him.

The <u>JERUSALEM POST</u> interviewed Prince Hassan at length, whom they named as, "one of the principle architects of the treaty," on October 29th, 2004. That happened to be the ten-year anniversary to the signing of the original Israeli-Jordanian peace treaty.

When Hassan was asked one interesting question, which pertained to how the negative public perceptions of the peace agreement, among the Jordanians, could be reversed, he said this: "Peace-building is a lot more challenging than peace-making...Peace-building and normal relations require time...As I have said before, it took Europe fifty years to arrive at the free movement of goods, capital, and labor. It will take <u>more than five or six years</u> to achieve full people-to-people peace in our region." [67]

Look at what he said, exactly. Not five years, not six years; that leaves seven years, doesn't it? That's his words. I think he chose them specifically when he was doing an interview with the <u>JERUSALEM POST</u>. Maybe you don't see any significance in that, but I sure do. Daniel says he shall confirm the covenant for how long? One week – seven years. El Hassan said, "It won't take five, and it won't take six." That leaves seven.

HIS SIGHTS ARE ON JERUSALEM

This one man, unlike any other man, has had his sight set upon one city – Jerusalem. In fact he believes that his very destiny is wrapped up within its future.

He wrote a book in 1979 entitled, "<u>A Study on Jerusalem</u>". In it he documents all historical facts, pertaining to the legal ramifications of past, present and future concerning this holy city of Jerusalem. He cites many numerous quotes, documents, U.N. resolutions, International declarations, religious traditions, Hague and Geneva Convention regulations, with nothing short of a brilliant intellect.

First of all, he concludes that Israel is in clear violation of the original General Assembly's Partition Plan Resolution of November, 1947. He concludes that the city of Jerusalem should actually be established as a *corpus seperatum*, or an "International City" that should be regulated and administered by UN Council. He also concludes that Israel is an "occupier of territories" and is in violation of world governing laws. He also concludes that all Holy Places, recognized by the three major religious bodies - Jewish, Muslim and Christian - must be protected and preserved by a new internationally recognized "guardian."

He also concludes that there should be an Arab Jerusalem, governed by a State of Palestine, as well as a Jewish Jerusalem, governed by Israel. He said this twenty-five years ago!

Do you realize that these are the exact same arguments now that everybody in the media uses, everybody who wants to know anything, or say anything, or get up and talk about it? We know these arguments don't have merit, but go check out what they're saying in the rest of the world. The world today believes this is the solution to the Jerusalem problem. El Hassan was the first person to articulate this position 25 years ago!

Lastly, he concludes that the overriding and overwhelming disputes concerning this city will require an "international interdependency" (Isn't that an interesting phrase?) "as the only way to achieve everlasting peace". That sounds like a cry for a world governing body or a world government.

In the very introduction of his book, he boldly and deliberately states that his presentation of these facts are important to him personally, because of his, "important part in Jerusalem's historical heritage," by merit of his, "Hashemite Kingdom" association.

From the outset, El Hassan is basically proclaiming, "I'm the man, because, after all, I've got historical heritage to Jerusalem because of my Hashemite lineage." [68]

Could he possibly be THE man…the man of sin?!

Quickly return to Daniel's prophetic words,

"And through his policy also he shall cause craft to prosper in his hand; and he shall magnify himself in his heart, and by peace shall destroy many." – Daniel 8:25:

Crown Prince El Hassan is personally committed to being a religious unifier, and to bringing the three major world religions, Jewish, Islam and Christianity together. He says it over, and over, and over again. Go to his personal website, and in five seconds you'll find it. He personally oversees numerous organizations founded for these Inter-Faith aims and goals, along with personally hosting and moderating gatherings which bring all religious leaders and expressions together for dialogue and cooperation and unity.

I have documented literally hundreds of speeches, actions and gatherings that are far too numerous to reveal within this book, in which El Hassan can be proven to be the single most influential spokesman for Inter-Faith goals to promote peace among all world religions. I know that's a bold statement, but it is easily proven.

The coming Man of Sin will have the satanic ability and the empowerment to unite <u>all religions</u> of the world together during the tribulation period, as described in Revelation 17 and 18. The very name and the place in the earth, which God identifies with this false religious system, is…Babylon!

January 28, 2004, at the New School University in New York, a forum entitled, *"A Muslim Centrist Platform for Democracy in the Arab World,"* was sponsored by "Dialogues," an organization for, "Islamic World – U.S. – and the West". This organization's board of advisors includes numerous political and religious luminaries from across the globe. Prince El Hassan gave the major presentation and was followed by a panel discussion, including: Prince El Hassan, Mustapha Tlili, who's the founder and director of "Dialogues," Bob Kerry, who is President of the University and former U.S. Senator, and none other than Steven Rockefeller.

Mustapha Tlili began the discussion by praising Prince Hassan for bringing hope to the "sad landscape" of the Arab world today. Tlili noted that the Prince's adherence to the values of tolerance, reason and human rights has been an inspiration for the Muslim people. Bob Kerry told the audience about the accomplishments of Prince Hassan, who has been honored by more than twenty countries and has risked his life over and over again for the sake of dialogue. Kerry welcomed the prince as a "friend of peace and freedom."

Steven Rockefeller made these perhaps prophetic comments: "Good evening. First of all, I'd like to express my profound gratitude to Prince El Hassan for accepting the invitation to share with us his courageous vision of a 'Muslim Centrist Platform for Democracy in the Arab World!' Prince El Hassan's branch of the Hashemite Family is directly descended from the Prophet Muhammad, and he occupies a unique place as a spiritual, social and political leader in the forty-second generation."

Steven Rockefeller continued to say this: "Your Royal Highness, your participation in this evening's dialogue provides all of us with a rare opportunity to deepen our understanding of the great spiritual tradition of Islam, the contemporary situation in the Arab world, and promising paths to democratic social change, human development, and peace in the Middle East and worldwide…As the world enters a global phase in development…the peoples and nations of the world have a choice.

"Under the influence of ancient prejudice, ignorance, and narrow self-interest, we can engage in a destructive clash of cultures and religions, or recognizing that we share a common humanity and planetary home, we can cooperate and support each other in building an equitable, sustainable and peaceful global society that respects cultural diversity and accepts pluralism. There is no greater social and spiritual challenge today than the pursuit of the latter goal in our local communities and globally."

"Tonight's dialogue on the future of the Arab world and on building better relations between the U.S. and the Islamic world is of central importance to this undertaking." [69]

This is very significant to me. Here you have a man on the level of Steven Rockefeller boldly praising Prince El Hassan as the man uniquely positioned to bring guidance in bringing a "peaceful, global society!"

During the final seven years, before the end of the age, a covenant is to be confirmed. If it was to be "confirmed" there would already have to be some form of a pre-existent document already in force; the pre-existing document must already be in place by some who have the position and authority to exercise the contents therein.

Daniel 9:26-27 says that the people of a coming prince would "confirm" a covenant. Here the Hebrew word that is used is *qum*. This word is always used when something prior is acknowledged, established, approved, or verified.

I want to give you quotes and statements by Prince El Hassan who I believe already established the right language in the peace treaty for these things to be fulfilled in Jerusalem and the covenant which he, himself, could confirm.

In his own words at the gathering of an award ceremony held at the Tanenbaum Center for Inter-Religious Understanding the Prince said, "I know I spent 30 years of my life in so-called secret negotiations with Yitzhak Rabin. It was a 'gentlemen's agreement'. You will say no to the right of return, and I will say yes to the right to return; and we'll all look good with our constituencies. But let's get on with the job of signing the peace, and moving from final status to permanent status!"

When I read this, an "alarm" began to go off. Let me reaffirm, a prince who has spent over 30 years of his political life in secret negotiations working on a peace process with the holy people, Israel.

The prince said that he wanted to make it clear that he would like to harness Muslim centrism in the cause of peace!

Since I believe that a possible candidate for the Antichrist will arise out of the territory of Jordan-Iraq, I believe that it is fair to say that as of the 25th day of July 1994, that the coming man of sin has already thereby established peace with Israel. As one report plainly puts it, Prince Hassan of Jordan is a veteran of a <u>thousand peace meetings</u> with Israel.

Remember the whole subject of the 70 weeks prophecy concerns "thy people" and "thy holy city", the holy people, referring to the nation of Israel. The peace has already been established, according to Daniel's prayer. There yet remains one outstanding issue as far as the seventy weeks are concerned. It is in fact the holy city, Jerusalem.

From Israel Ministry of Foreign Affairs, Ruth Lapidot wrote on Jerusalem, "It is generally thought that Jerusalem is the most difficult problem that the peace-makers have to deal with. The centrality of the issue of Jerusalem derives neither from security considerations nor from economic interests, but from emotional and religious sensitivities. The complexity of the issue is the result of three factors.

"The city is holy for adherents of Christianity, Islam and Judaism, namely, it is sacred for many millions of people, most of whom do not live in the city. It is the subject of conflicting national claims of two peoples--Israelis and Palestinian Arabs; and its population is very heterogeneous. A solution to the conflicts about Jerusalem is a *sin qua non* for the achievement of a viable and durable peace in the area." [70]

In the book of 2 Chronicles 6:6,7:16,33:7 reads I [God] have chosen Jerusalem, that my name might be there…for now I have chosen and sanctified this house [the temple], that my name may be there perpetually…in this house and Jerusalem, which I have chosen…I will put my name forever. For the Lord has chosen Zion he has desired it for his dwelling place. (Psalm 132:13)

And it shall be in that day, I will seek to destroy all the nations that come against Jerusalem. (Zechariah 12:9)

For King David Jerusalem was a place of extreme joy and passion. Nowhere is this more expressed, than when he writes in Psalm 137:5-6,

"If I forget thee, O Jerusalem, let my right hand forget her cunning. If I do not remember thee, let my tongue cleave to the roof of my mouth; if I prefer not Jerusalem above my chief joy." – Psalm 137:5-6

Jerusalem is very special to one other person. His name is His Royal Highness Prince El Hassan bin Talal. He even wrote a book, written in 1979 entitled, "A Study on Jerusalem," of which I have referred to previously. To say that the Prince has some knowledge of the Jerusalem issues would be a gross understatement. Prince Hassan has a fixation on Jerusalem that he seems to have been born with. His knowledge of the holy city is second to none.

Any discussion of Jordanian policy must recall that, given his Shariffian lineage, the late King Hussein was regarded as a descendent of the Prophet Muhammad; his family exercised a religious role as caretakers of Mecca and Medina in the 1920's.

Jordan's political control over the eastern parts of Jerusalem ended in 1967, but its religious role continued nonetheless. The Israeli government left the functions of religious affairs under the East Jerusalem Waqf from the Jordanian administration. Thus, the Jordanian Ministry of Awqaf (Waqf) and not the Israeli Ministry of Religious Affairs managed the matters of the East Jerusalem Waqf.

The Waqf existed under Jordanian law and Jordan appointed its officials, who generally came from pro-Jordanian segments of the Palestinian Arab population. More recent tensions between Jordan and the Palestinians in this regard are detailed below.

Jordan provided considerable funding to the Waqf as well. The relative role of Jordan in the Waqf budget increased over the years: in 1977, for example, Waqf expenditures of 951,356 dinars came from Waqf income of 382,389 dinars and a Jordanian contribution of 568,967 dinars. By 1982, as Waqf expenditures increased to 2,607,486 dinars, the relative contribution of Waqf income fell to 362,437 dinars, while the Jordanian contribution rose to 2,245,049 dinars. [71]

Jordan's decision of July 31, 1988, to sever the Hashemite Kingdom's administrative ties to the West Bank did not affect the connections of its Ministry of Religious Endowments and Religious Affairs to the Waqf. These connections continued into 1994. King Hussein allotted about 8 million dollars for repair work on the Temple Mount mosques.

Jordan's policy regarding Jerusalem went through significant developments due to the DOP. King Hussein reconfirmed his kingdom's responsibility for the Islamic holy sites in the eastern parts of the city. His public statements indicated a willingness to look at the issue of Jerusalem as primarily as religious issue: "With regard to the Islamic holy places of Jerusalem in particular, our position remains unchanged…We did not, nor will we ever, recognize any sovereignty over them except by almighty God, as indeed with the holy places of all believers in God in this most holy city."

A day after signing the Israeli-Jordanian Peace Treaty, in October 1994, former Crown Prince Hassan added new elements to the definition of Jordan's role in Jerusalem.

He explained on November 1 that Jordan exercised "holy authority" or "moral authority" over holy shrines within the walls of the Old City. Yet the Jordanian role was now circumscribed in time: *"In the final status negotiations, when jurisdiction (over the Old City) is transferred to the Palestinian side, this responsibility in its entirely will be transferred to those concerned."* He stated that current arrangements were for the interim period alone.

Two elements could be inferred from Hassan's statement.

First, while expressing a willingness to modify the current interim arrangements in the holy places, Hassan only stated that Jordan's responsibility for holy sites would be transferred "to those concerned;" he did not make explicit reference to a Palestinian Authority. Jordan could still fit into the category of a concerned party.

Second, by stating that present arrangements would be modified only if a final status territorial settlement was reached between Israel and the Palestinians, Jordan now conceivably had an interest in final status agreements never being reached.

Both of these possibilities were contained in statements by then Prime Minister 'Abd al-Salin al-Majali to MBC on October 30, 1994, *"As to what the final solution will be, there will be a role for Jordan in any final solution."* In other words, we shall submit our viewpoint when the issue is resolved in the final phase. "On Jordan's behalf, I affirm to you that on the day when Israel's political sovereignty over Jerusalem ends and the brother Palestinians take over sovereignty, we shall seriously consider abandoning this jurisdiction." [72]

Neither Crown Prince Hassan nor Prime Minister al-Majali precluded a continuing Jordanian religious role in the final status. They opened up the possibility that the claims of others could be considered.

Under King Abdullah, Jordanian efforts to come to a *modus vivendi* with the PLO have accelerated and insistence on retaining Jordan's exclusive role has been modified. Not long after taking office, in May 1999, Abdullah still referred to Jordan being a partner in determining the final status of Jerusalem, *"Well, Jerusalem is extremely important to me as a Hashemite, as a Muslim, as a Jordanian. And I believe that whether we reach final status discussions that I hope that Jordan will have a voice on the future of Jerusalem."* King Abdullah did not speak specifically about the Washington Declaration and Jordan's special role as caretaker of the mosques on the Temple Mount.

Abdullah's prime minister, Abdul-Raouf al-Rawabdeh, dropped the Jordanian claim to Jerusalem's holy sites altogether in August 1999. He stated that Jordan was willing to turn over its control of these sites to the PLO. By November 1999, Abdullah was willing to give unqualified support for making Jerusalem the capital of a Palestinian state. However, formal pronouncements in this regard can be expected to shift with the vicissitudes of the process. [73]

The one who will come, who is given the power to "confirm" this covenant has to be someone who was involved with the initial covenant and not just "any one". Keep in mind also that in order for him to fulfill the prophecy of Daniel 11:39, where he shall "divide" the land for gain or for a price he must exercise some kind of legitimate authority over this area.

"Thus shall he do in the most strong holds with a strange god, whom he shall acknowledge and increase with glory: and he shall cause them to rule over many, and shall divide the land for gain. – *Daniel 11:39*

Only the Islamic Hashemites, through the vehicle of modern Jordan, can claim to have the authority to control and influence the holy site of the Temple Mount, and any "division" of Jerusalem!

Remember the key issue that will start Daniel's seventh week or the final seven years is Jerusalem and the holy people, the Jews.

The Man of Sin

Let's look at the Bible one more time,

"And after threescore and two weeks shall Messiah be cut off, but not for himself: and the people of the prince that shall come shall destroy the city and the sanctuary; and the end thereof shall be with a flood, and unto the end of the war desolations are determined. And he shall confirm the covenant with many for one week: and in the midst of the week he shall cause the sacrifice and the oblation to cease, and for the overspreading of abominations he shall make it desolate, even until the consummation, and that determined shall be poured upon the desolate." – *Daniel 9:26-27*

That phrase "the people of the prince who is to come" is quite something. Many scholars see this as a reference to a Roman prince. And they see a "revived Roman Empire" as being the seat of the Antichrist's power. So how does an Arab-Hashemite fit in? First of all, in Daniel's interpretation of Nebuchadnezzar's dream, the final empire, was portrayed by the legs of the statue. This is Rome, of course, divided between Western and Eastern branches. The Eastern branch, centered in Constantinople (Istanbul), was comprised primarily of the lands that later fell to the Prophet Mohammed's conquering sword…

"He shall confirm the covenant with many for one week." Other translations have it that he shall "confirm a covenant." This is an interesting passage. Prince El Hassan has already proposed a treaty between Israel and the Arabs that would need to last about seven years for peace to "take." The idea of "confirming" a covenant is interesting, too. It would suggest that something is already in place. Perhaps it is. Remember, El Hassan was the behind-the-scenes architect of the Oslo Accords. A confirmation of that agreement may be all that is necessary to bring a false peace into existence.

Looking farther into the career of the Antichrist we find that he shall come as a man of peace, and later, as Daniel 8:25 tells us, *"by peace shall destroy many."* Revelation tells us that the reign of the man of sin will involve a One World Government animated and supported by a One World Religion. Prince El Hassan is the biggest promoter of religious unity. Besides acting as President of the Club of Rome, he is involved with the United Nations' Commission on Refugees, the Foundation for Interreligious and Intercultural Research and Dialaogue, the Council on Foreign Relations and he is the President of the Center for Peace Studies.

In fact, the Prince's entire message is peace and tolerance. According to El Hassan, what is needed is "an ethic of human solidarity and a new international order." His overriding goal is "interfaith dialogue" that will repair the rift between the three great monotheistic, Abrahamic religions: Judaism, Christianity and Islam. Remember that through his family ties to both the Sunni and Shiite factions, he is ideally placed to serve as a peacemaker within Islam. Viewing himself as a key cog in the peacemaking process, and his destiny as being somehow tied in to Jerusalem, Prince El Hassan has come out in favor of that Holy City coming under international joint control by representatives of the three faiths.

Daniel 9:27 tells us the Antichrist will put an end to the daily sacrifices. That must mean they will have been reinstated first. Jewish tradition tells us that the Temple will be rebuilt when Messiah comes. There are organizations in Israel right now preparing the artifacts for a rebuilt Temple. They expect the soon coming of Messiah. The Antichrist will be instrumental in reestablishing the Judaic religious system. Notably the Hashemite family regained "religious authority" over the Temple Mount back in 2004.

The agreement between Israel and Jordan states, "Israel respects the present special role of the Hashemite Kingdom of Jordan in Muslim holy shrines in Jerusalem." That means a candidate from the Hashemite family is uniquely placed to broker peace between Palestinians and Jews. He will be just as uniquely qualified to set up and put an end to the sacrifice (Daniel 9:27) and "sitteth in the temple of God" as God. (2 Thessalonians 2:4)

In this book, I have developed several threads of evidence that point to the **_POSSIBILITY_** that Prince El Hassan is uniquely qualified to assume the role of Antichrist or Mahdi. He fulfills the prophetic requirements. He must be:

1. A Gentile Muslim – He is.
2. An Assyrian – He is.
3. King of Babylon – He is in line for Iraqi throne.
4. Man of Peace – He is.
5. Peacemaker with Israel – He penned the Oslo Accords.
6. Promoter of Religious Unity – He is.
7. Claims to Jerusalem – through Hashemites.
8. Known as the Mahdi – He qualifies.

Only Prince El Hassan of Jordan fulfills all of these prophetic requirements!

I think many prophecy preachers over the years have mistakenly taught and wrongly taught that this Man of Sin is going to come in like an Adolph Hitler, and come in like a Saddam Hussein, and come in like a Yasser Arafat. No – He's going to come in with the best intentions the world has ever known or seen. He comes in with a heart that he thinks is pure. But in the middle of the Tribulation, Lucifer, himself, finds something in his heart, and seizes it within his heart. He yields himself to Lucifer. Then he becomes what we know as "the Man of Sin." He doesn't start out that way.

BIBLICAL CONCLUSIONS

The prophetic scriptures make these conclusions in identifying the "man of sin":

- The coming Man of Sin will be a Gentile Muslim.

- The coming Man of Sin will be from the region of ancient Assyria.

- The coming Man of Sin will be a prince.

- The coming Man of Sin will be the king of Babylon (Iraq).

- The coming man of Sin will enter the world scene as a man of peace.

- The coming Man of Sin will be a peacemaker with Israel.

- The coming Man of Sin will seek to bring the world's religions together.

- The coming Man of Sin will lay claim to Jerusalem.

- The coming Man of Sin will allow Jordan to escape from his military might.

- Lastly, the coming Man of Sin will be known as the Mahdi to the Islamic world!

There is only **ONE MAN** on the world scene today who can meet all of these identifying signs!

Some students of Bible Prophecy will fail to see the significance of this book. They'll even reject it all as "mere conjecture". They may even attempt to discredit me, or at least declare that, *"No one will ever really know who the Man of Sin will be."* I've heard that, and you have, too. And, that's fine. For in time, all of us will know the truth.

As I conclude, let me assure you of God's Biblical promise,

*"Ye are of God, little children, and have overcome them: because **greater is he that is in you, than he that is in the world**."* – 1 John 4:4

The context here is the spirit of Antichrist. He says, "You, little children, have <u>overcome</u> them." We don't fear this man! We don't fear this end-time Antichrist spirit!

Do not fear the Antichrist, because <u>greater</u> is He that is in you than He that is in the world!

"Be ye therefore ready also: for in such an hour that ye think not, the Son of man cometh."

Twelfth Imam Could Appear This Spring, Says Iran!

Iranian TV series explains signs of the "last days," suggests apocalyptic war against Jews and Christians could come in 2007.
By Joel C. Rosenberg
(WASHINGTON, D.C., January 2, 2007)

The New Year may not be so happy if Iranian leaders have their way.

The Islamic Messiah known as the "Twelfth Imam" or the "Mahdi" may come to earth in 2007 and could be revealed to the world as early as the Spring Equinox, reports an official Iranian government news website. The Islamic Republic of Iran Broadcasting (IRIB) website says the world is now in its "last days." It claims that the Mahdi will first appear in Mecca, and then Medina. He will conquer all of Arabia, Syria, Iraq, destroy Israel, and then set up a "global government" based in Iraq, interestingly enough, not Iran. Such Islamic eschatology (end times theology) is driving the Iranian regime and helps explains why Iran has no interest in helping the U.S. and E.U. create peace in Iraq or the region, much less in ending its bid for nuclear weapons, the Iraq Study Group Report notwithstanding.

Anticipation of the imminent arrival or "illumination" of the Islamic Messiah has been steadily intensifying inside Iran since Mahmoud Ahmadinejad emerged as president of the country in June of 2005. A television series on IRIB called "The World Towards Illumination" has been running since last November to help answer the many questions Iranians have about the end of the world as we know it. The series explains the signs of the last days and what to expect when the Islamic Messiah arrives. The program also says that Jesus is coming back to earth soon as a Shiite Muslim leader and it denounces "born again Christians" for supporting "the illegal Zionist state of Israel." An Israeli news site was the first to pick up the story and its significance to Israeli national security, noting that the Mahdi will soon "form an army to defeat Islam's enemies in a series of apocalyptic battles" and "will overcome his archvillain in Jerusalem."

Some intelligence analysts are growing concerned by Ahmadinejad's announced plans "to hold the big celebration of Iran's full nuclearization in the current year." Iran's calendar year ends on March 20, which is the usual date of the Spring Equinox. Is Ahmadinejad signaling that Iran will have nuclear weapons by then? Is he suggesting that an apocalyptic war to annihilate Jews and Christians in Israel and the U.S. and could come in 2007, perhaps as early as this spring or summer? It is not yet clear, though Ahmadinejad today vowed to "humiliate" the U.S. and continues to vow that Israel is to "vanish" soon.

The Iranian TV series is important in that it offers

some intriguing clues as to how Iranian Shiites believe their prophecies will play out. "After [the Twelfth Imam's] uprising from Mecca all of Arabia will be submit to him and then other parts of the world as he marches upon Iraq and established his seat of global government in the city of Kufa. Then the Imam will send 10 thousand of his forces to the east and west to uproot the oppressors. At this time God will facilitate things for him and lands will come under his control one after the other…He will appear as a handsome young man, clad in neat clothes and exuding the fragrance of paradise. His face will glow with love and kindness for the human beings…He has a radiant forehead, black piercing eyes and a broad chest. He very much resembles his ancestor Prophet Mohammad. Heavenly light and justice accompany him. He will overcome enemies and oppressors with the help of God, and as per the promise of the Almighty the Mahdi will eradicate all corruption and injustice from the face of the earth and establish the global government of peace, justice and equity."

The TV series notes that "in our discussion of the world in the last days of the earth we had said in our previous editions of this program that no source has pointed to the exact date when the Savior will appear and only God knows about the exact timing of the reappearance of Imam Mahdi…There are various versions of the exact day of his reappearance. Some say it would be Friday and the date will be Ashura or the 10th of Moharram, the heart-rending martyrdom anniversary of his illustrious ancestor, Imam Husain. Others say the date will be the 25th of the month of Zil-Qa'dah and may coincide with the Spring Equinox or Nowrooz as the Iranians call. A saying attributed to the Prophet's 6th infallible heir, Imam Ja'far Sadeq (PBUH) says the Mahdi will appear on the Spring Equinox and God will make him defeat Dajjal the Impostor or the anti-Christ as the Christians say, who will be hanged near the dump of Kufa."

Before the Islamic Messiah appears to the world, IRIB reports, "a pious person…a venerable God-fearing individual from Iran" meets with the Mahdi. This individual will pledge allegiance to the Mahdi as he "fights oppression and corruption and enters Iraq to lift the siege of Kufa and holy Najaf and to defeat the forces of [Islam's enemies] in Iraq." It is not clear whether the program is referring to President Ahmadinejad or someone to come.

Shiite Islamic scholars also say Jesus is coming back to Earth soon. He will not, however, come as the Son of God or even as a leader but will serve as a deputy to the Mahdi to destroy the infidels, such scholars say. "We read in the book Tazkarat ol-Olia, 'the Mahdi will come with Jesus son of Mary accompanying him,'" the series explains. "This indicates that these two great men are to complement each other. Imam Mahdi will be the leader while Prophet Jesus will act as his lieutenant in the struggle against oppression and establishment of justice in the world."

"The apocalypse is a deep belief among humans regarding the end of the world," notes the Iranian documentary. "[O]ne of the characteristics of the West in the current era is obsession with the end of time. Experts say discussions about the savior and the 'end of time', have not been so prevalent before as they are now in the west....They believe the Messiah [is Jesus and that He] will reappear and will establish his global rule with its center in [Jerusalem], with the help of born again Christians. This sect's religious leaders in the 1990's strongly propagated their beliefs in the US and European societies. In the past two years dozens of books have been published in this field…These extremist Christians believe that certain events must be carried out by the Protestants in the world so as to prepare the grounds for the Messiah's reappearance. The followers of this school believe they have a religious duty to accelerate these events, for example planting the illegal Zionist state of Israel for the Jews of the world, in Palestine."

Too many Western analysts are missing the central importance of Shiite eschatology in Iranian foreign policy. They mistakenly believe that Iran's current leadership can be somehow cajoled into making peace with the West. Nothing could be further from the truth. Mahmoud Ahmadinejad and his cadre of loyal mullahs are not being driven by the same goals and aspirations as are the diplomats in Washington, Brussels or at the United Nations. The President of Iran and his team fervently believe the Islamic Messiah is coming back soon, possibly as soon as this Spring. They are convinced that their divine mission is to create the conditions for the Mahdi's return. As a result, they are committed to instigating more anti-American violence in Iraq, not less. They are determined to obtain nuclear weapons at all costs, not negotiate away their atomic research and development program. What's more, they are deeply committed to building political and military alliances with anti-Western powers, not finding accommodation with the West.

Bottom line: the leaders of Iran are preparing for an apocalyptic war with the U.S. and Israel. It's not a question of "if" but "when." The sooner the White House and our new Congressional leaders realize this and take decisive action to stop this nuclear nightmare, the better. [74]

APPENDIX A

Contrasting CHRIST with *Antichrist*:

1. Jesus is the Son of God (John 1:34)
    Antichrist is the son of perdition
    (meaning "destruction") (II Thessalonians 2:3)

2. Jesus is the Seed of the Woman (Genesis 3:15)
    Antichrist is the seed of the serpent (Genesis 3:15)

3. Jesus is the Lamb (Isaiah 53:7)
    Antichrist is the beast (Revelation 11:7)

4. Jesus is the Holy One (Mark 1:24)
    Antichrist is the wicked one (II Thessalonians 2:8)

5. Jesus is the Truth (John 14:6)
    Antichrist is the lie (John 8:44)

6. Jesus is the Prince of Peace (Isaiah 9:6)
    Antichrist is the profane wicked prince (Ezekiel 21:25)

7. Jesus is the Glorious Branch (Isaiah 4:2)
    Antichrist is the abominable branch (Isaiah 14: 19)

8. Jesus is the mighty Angel (Revelation 10:1)
    Antichrist is the angel of the bottomless pit
    (Revelation 9:11)

9. Jesus is the Good Shepherd, who leads His flocks (John 10:3)
   Antichrist is the idol shepherd, who neglects his flocks (Zechariah 11:17)

10. Jesus came in God's Name (John 5:43)
    Antichrist will come in his own name (John 5:43)

11. Jesus cleansed the Temple (John 2:15)
    Antichrist will defile the Temple (Matthew 24:15)

12 Jesus was slain for the people (John 11:51)
   Antichrist will slay the people (Isaiah 14:20)

MORE STATEMENTS ON JERUSALEM
BY PRINCE EL HASSAN

From an unnamed source, Prince Hassan said "Jerusalem is a Palestinian matter" and "We support the establishment of a Palestinian state with Jerusalem as a capital."

The prince said, "What is of concern to us in the negotiations are the Islamic Awgaf (Islamic trusts) and the holy shrines which will be handed over to the Palestinians so as to crown the Palestinian responsibility. "This is the first time a Jordanian official has announced" that Jordan will give up the administration of the Islamic shrines in Jerusalem to the Palestinians.

In Casablanca, Prince Hassan of Jordan on Tuesday the 1st of November, 2006, stated that, *"Jordan will hand over Jerusalem shrines to Palestinians when they reach final accord"* on Jerusalem.

JERUSALEM: JOY OF THE WHOLE EARTH

Address by His Royal Highness Prince El Hassan upon the announcement of his appointment as President of The Club of Rome.

"In this common human privilege (which we all share) there are not privacies and not monopolies, no exclusive holiness, no peculiar peoples' only distinctive races climates, living spaces and environment and a rich diversity of cultures all under God in an equal benediction and at a comparable risk to their 'ever generous Lord'. The excellence of Jerusalem is to

have been, and to remain, one (redoubtable) of such capital cities summoned as such to be the JOY OF THE WHOLE EARTH." [75]

One other thing to note, Prince Hassan is not saying, "Maybe" or "If," but "Jordan, in fact, will hand over the Jerusalem shrines to Palestinians when they reach final accord on Jerusalem."

Remember, Jesus said when you see the abomination of desolation which was spoken of by Daniel, that prophet standing in the holy place for the one reading, let him understanding, then let those in Judea flee to the mountains. (Matthew 24: 15; 16 JP Greens Literal Translation)

A question was raised in an article in 1992, in the Jerusalem Report Magazine's 10th Anniversary, to Prince Hassan about the book he wrote on the legal status of Jerusalem published in 1979. He was asked if he considered the suggestion he offered in the book still workable?

Here is Prince Hassan's answer, "I haven't changed my view one iota. The first element is the one of a *corpus separatus* regarding the holy places, and that doesn't apply to Jerusalem alone, but to other sites like those in Bethlehem as well. That's an issue that cannot be addressed in public because of the high emotions involved. In a way, it is succumbed to the second issue of political sovereignty and the Palestinian-Israeli issue. The third point is the municipalities where they would be. The basic issue is, however, the territories occupied in 1967. In the period of an interim settlement in the territories, will Jordan remain in charge of the Waqf (the Muslim Religious Council in Jerusalem), Al-Aqsa Mosque and so on? This is a basic pillar of the whole Muslim world. Jordan has to continue to shoulder the responsibility for this." [76]

These statements are taken from Crown Prince El Hassan's book, *A Study on Jerusalem.*

INTRODUCTION TO A STUDY ON JERUSALEM

The Hashemite Kingdom of Jordan's association with the Holy City is an important part of its historic heritage, as well as an article of faith for all its people. The grave, in Jerusalem, of Sherif Hussein bin Ali, the leader of the Arab Revolt, bears witness to his commitment to the cause of Palestine. The Kingdom's founder, the late King Abdullah, lost his life on the steps of the Al-Aqsa Mosque, a fact not unrelated to his championing of freedom and justice in the Holy Land. My father, the late King Talal fought for Palestinian Arab rights in Jerusalem. His Majesty King Hussein has repeatedly invited a consensus of believers in God to work towards addressing the complexities of this potentially unifying, yet tragically divisive, problem.

This Study takes a first step towards a clarification of the background on questions of sovereignty, as well as municipal rights and control of the Holy Places. It is the hope of those associated with this initiative that objectivity should be maintained throughout. I have borne in mind "that Truth often suffers more by the heat of its defenders, than from the arguments of its opposers."

1. It is manifest that the acutely difficult question of the future status of Jerusalem is not likely to be resolved by exclusive attention to the legal issues. These issues, in themselves, present formidable uncertainties. As in all

major international issues, their legal aspects cannot be ignored. Neither can they of themselves afford solutions. Thus it is that any attempted analysis of the legal questions can be no more than one element in the overall effort to resolve the solution of the Jerusalem question in a way that will promote both peace and justice.

2. As has been pointed out by Michael Brecher in an article written in the <u>Middle East Journal</u> in 1978, *"All plans for Jerusalem will remain moribund until an Arab-Israel accommodation is reached: the struggle for Jerusalem is inextricably linked to an overall settlement. It remains to note that Israel's decision-makers have recognized a near-universal external opposition to their decision and actions on Jerusalem."* Matters have become, if anything, even more complex and fast moving since he wrote those words. There has been no dearth of proposals for the future of Jerusalem, whether on the State, Municipal, or religio-functional level. As yet, none of them has evoked that desire to reach a compromise between the contesting parties without which no lasting solution is feasible. The three critical and divisive legal elements in the Jerusalem Solution have been and still are today, sovereignty, municipal government and the control of the Holy Places within and outside Jerusalem. It is with these three key elements that this Study will be primarily concerned, treating them from the legal perspectives. There are undoubtedly numerous other divisive legal issues that would have to be resolved by compromise, but until some accommodation can be made on those three topics a successful compromise or settlement is unlikely.

3. The U.N. is as strong and as weak as its Members wish to make it. At the moment, there may be some hesitancy

in accepting the claims of the PLO, but the pattern of relationships in and outside the Middle East is changing rapidly. It is as yet unknown whether the principle of self-determination will develop as a legal base for political settlements, supported by the international community.

The principal of self-determination of peoples, as now interpreted, has its roots in justice as far back as the Mandate. It may well afford a legal basis for peace in the area. The future juridical status of Jerusalem would prove a major stumbling block (What was King Hussian's stand on Jordan?) to any such arrangements. In that city the principle of self-determination of peoples would probably afford no solution.

4. The alternative view would be the following questions and answers put forward by Lord Caradon in August of 1979: *"Was East Jerusalem occupied by Israel in the 1967 War?"* Of course it was. Was the United Nations Resolution 242 intended to apply to occupied East Jerusalem? Of course it was. Nor is this issue of East Jerusalem academic, remote or unreal. It is, as I say, fundamental, immediate, overriding." He continues, in his "proposed draft resolution of the U.N. General Assembly" to say: "There should be an Arab Jerusalem and an Israeli Jerusalem each exercising full sovereignty within its own territory" (i.e., Israel and the new Arab State of Palestine), but with no barriers between them and no impediment in freedom of movement between them."

Under Lord Caradon's proposal each State would enjoy sovereignty over its own part of Jerusalem, (determined under U.N. auspices). Lord Caradon further proposes: "The resolution might also request the Secretary General to appoint a representative to be stationed in Jerusalem not to administer the City. That would be for the Israelis on one side and the Palestinians on the other; but to work with all concerned to secure the purposes of the resolution, particularly for the preservation of the holy places and free access to them." Thus, each part of the City would be a separate enclave within the territory of each state. The inter-religious, ecumenical regime, distinct from the two State sovereignties, would operate within and outside Jerusalem and be determined by an international statute under U.N. auspices.

Perhaps the time has come and gone when the parties to the Jerusalem controversy can be content with the rehearsal of past grievances and current legal claims to territorial sovereignty. Solution by resort to armed conflict has shown that military success produces, for the victor, insecurity and a mounting climate of hostile reaction from the community of States. The overriding needs inherent in international interdependency may achieve more for the peace and well-being of the Middle East than the contesting claims of State sovereignty, the recital of grievances and the obdurate preservation of the sad realities of today.

5. "We see no contradiction whatsoever between Israel's sovereignty in New Jerusalem and the satisfaction of international requirements concerning such Holy Places as are located within it; insofar as there is here a practical problem to be solved, it can only be solved on the basis of a clear distinction between the status of Jerusalem as a city and a capital and the status of the Holy Places,"

In fact, since the war of June, 1967, and the enactment of, Israel considers itself as "the present guardian" of the

Israel Protection of Holy Places Law on June 27, 1967. Israel considers itself as "the present guardian of the Holy Places in the Old City," and is willing to co-operate with the leaders of the three religious communities. This posture overlooks the juridical status of Israel in that area, i.e., an Occupant that has denied any annexation of the Old City and its extended suburbs. It is, of course, a reply to any proposals to place the whole City under an international regime as a *corpus separatum*; distinct from the State of Israel or of Jordan. The question of the Holy Places is for Israel a weak point in its claim that Jerusalem is, for religious and historical reasons, destined to be the capital and religious centre of the Jewish State for ever. Its religious claims are not unique but are shared with two other religions, over a long period of time, with many millions of adherents in the contemporary world. Much emphasis has been laid by Israeli apologists upon the unsatisfactory nature of international regimes. They point to the terms of the Protection of Holy Places Law, 1967, and their policy of safeguarding free access to, and worship at, the Holy Places now under Israel's control. What they fail to point out is that, at least so far as the Old City is concerned, where the majority of the more important Holy Places are situated, Israel has no territorial sovereignty, but only the status of an Occupant with temporary, limited authority subject to legal obligations imposed upon it by the Hague Regulations of 1907 and the Geneva (Fourth) Convention of 1949.

6. From 638 A.D. until now the Christians have shared a religious presence with the Muslims; the Jewish religious presence, with the Muslims. The Jewish religious

presence, apart from vertigial practioners of the Jewish faith, was absent from 135 A.D. until the 19th century. Thus, the tripartite religious presence of the three great monotheist religions of the world in Jerusalem is less than two centuries old. The rights of accession, and worship at the Holy Places within and outside Jerusalem are shared, and not exclusive, rights.

The biblical claim to the territory of Palestine, "Eretz" Israel, as advanced by Mr. Begin, other Israeli Ministers and contemporary Jewish apologists, is equally unconvincing. The biblical texts are not consistent about God's promises to Abraham. The Bible's historical accuracy varies. Records exist in neighboring countries, such as a powerful nation before the time of Solomon, and the only for a brief period.

The true nature of the Jewish historical-religious claim to Jerusalem can perhaps be seen in the words of Dayan before the Wailing Wall on the afternoon of 7 June, 1967:

"We have returned to this most sacred shrine, never to part from it." Any association during a period of the last 1800 years, marked by the Jewish yearning to return to Jerusalem, is not an historical or a territorial association. Neither does it afford a persuasive title to territorial sovereignty under contemporary international law. [77]

This book was written 28 years ago and 15 years before a peace treaty was reached with Israel.

SPEECH TO THE
EUROPEAN-ATLANTIC GROUP 11-20-03

Here are excerpts of a speech given by Crown Prince El Hassan to the European-Atlantic Group on November 20, 2003.

"I think that the prediction of two remarks I made earlier on is upon a change of policy, a major shift in policy, a definite timeline for withdrawal from Iraq, responsibility for legitimate Iraqi authority, a change of policy to involve – includes to create inclusion of an 'intra-independent' Benelux with a new road map. Whereby three intra-independent states complement each other: Jordan, Palestine and Israel."

"You might like to ask, 'What has Jordan got to do with it?' I'll tell you: it has quite a lot to do with it. We signed a solemn peace treaty in which we made it very clear that the current state of negotiations between Palestinians and Israelis reflects Palestinians and Israelis particularities in the context of final status. Final status, to endure, should be followed by permanent-status talks on trans-boundary issues such as refugees, Jerusalem and regional communities of water and energy, something that I would very much endorse." [78]

JERUSALEM'S HOLY PLACE
AND THE PEACE PROCESS

By Marshall J. Broger and Thomas A. Idinopulos. Policy Paper Series NO. 46 Washington, D.C.: The Washington Institute for Near East Policy, 1998.

Prince Hassan bin Talal, brother of the late King Hussein and former Crown Prince of Jordan, concluded his study on Jerusalem and the Holy Places in the following words: "Perhaps the time has come and gone when the parties to Jerusalem controversy can be content with the rehearsal of past grievances and current legal claims to territorial sovereignty. Solution by resort to armed conflict has shown that Military success produces, for the victor, insecurity and a mounting climate of hostile reaction from community states. The overriding needs inherent to international interdependency may achieve more for the peace and well being of the Middle East than the contesting claims of State Sovereignty, the recital of grievances and the obdurate preservation of the sad reality of today (A Study on Jerusalem)." [79]

The report went on to conclude, that since Prince Hassan wrote these words, two decades ago, Jordan and Israel have concluded a peace treaty while Israel and the PLO reached mutual recognition and entered an ongoing negotiation process.

VATICAN COMMENDS KING HUSSEIN AND CROWN PRINCE EL HASSAN

The Vatican reaffirmed its support for the efforts made by King Hussein and Crown Prince El Hassan towards the establishment of peace in the Middle East and for encouraging dialogue among the three monotheistic faiths, securing free worship and protecting human rights, The Vatican's views were conveyed by the charge d'affairs stressed the Vatican's outright rejection of Israel's claims to the Holy City as its capital, arguing that Jerusalem should be open for all and no one should claim sovereignty.

PRINCE HASSAN CHANGES THE KING'S MIND

Clement Henry notes in his profile of Prince Hassan dated the 21st of November 1996. He writes: *"The Prince's role goes beyond that of an emissary, however, for he also plays an increasingly important function as a policy maker. For example, it was his statement regarding Jordan's commitment to the Muslim Holy Sights in Jerusalem that in fact changed King Hussein's stance on the issue."* [80]

How significant is that?

LIVING ON BORROWED TIME

Joan Van Wessel, from the <u>Jerusalem Report</u> passed to Prince Hassan a question in the Jerusalem report, "Your Highness, you mentioned a Russian terrorism expert who said that Sharif had to be contained. Isn't the lack of real separation between church and state one of the problems in the Arab and Islamic works?"

Prince Hassan responded, "We need to legitimate religion with (a Vatican in Jerusalem,) A Vatican Mecca, a Vatican in Najaf, the seat of Shicism. When I saw Shimon Peres a few months ago, I asked. 'Why does the Israeli ministry approve a license for the building of a Mosque outside the Basilica in Nazareth?' It is the beginning of a rift between Christians and Muslims. We do not need that." [81]

From The Jordan Webpage…
JORDANIAN POLICY ON JERUSALEM

Jordan's policy regarding Jerusalem went through significant developments due to the DOP. King Hussein reconfirmed his kingdom's responsibility for the Islamic holy sites in the eastern parts of the city. His public statements indicated a willingness to look at the issue of Jerusalem as primarily a religious issue: "With regard to the Islamic holy places of Jerusalem in particular, our position remains unchanged….We did not, nor will we ever, recognize any sovereignty over them, except by almighty God, as indeed with the holy places of all believers in God in this most holy city." A day after signing the Israeli-Jordanian Peace Treaty in October 1994, Former Crown Prince Hasan added new elements to the definition of Jordan's role in Jerusalem.

He explained on November 1 that Jordan exercised "holy authority" or "moral authority" over holy shrines within the walls of the Old City. Yet the Jordanian role was now circumscribed in time: "in the final status negotiations, when jurisdiction (over the Old City) is transferred to the Palestinian side, this responsibility in its entirely will be transferred to those concerned." He stated that current arrangements were for the interim period alone.

Two elements could be inferred from Hassan's statement. First, while expressing a willingness to modify the current interim arrangements in the holy places, Hassan only stated that Jordan's responsibility for holy sites would be transferred to those concerned; he did not make explicit reference to a Palestinian authority. Jordan could still fit into the category of a concerned party.

Second, by stating that present arrangements would be modified only if a final status territorial settlement was reached between Israel and the Palestinians, Jordan now conceivably had an interest in final status agreements never being reached.

Both of these possibilities were contained in statements by then Prime Minister 'Abd al-Salim al-Majali to MBC on October 30, 1994: "As to what the final solution will be, there will be a role for Jordan in any final solution. In other words, we shall submit our viewpoint when the issue is resolved in the final phase. On Jordan's behalf, I affirm to you that on the day when Israel's political sovereignty over Jerusalem ends and the brother Palestinians take over sovereignty, we shall seriously consider abandoning this jurisdiction." Thus, neither Crown Prince Hassan nor Prime Minister al-Majali precluded a continuing Jordanian religious role in the final status. They opened up the possibility that the claims of others could be considered. [82]

According to **FOXNEWS**, at a Jerusalem news conference, Labor lawmaker Yossi Beilin, an architect of the breakthrough 1993 Israel-PLO accord, warned Israelis and Palestinians they were heading for violence and urged postponing the May 1999 deadline for a final peace accord. Arafat has vowed to declare a Palestinian state on the West Bank and Gaza Strip in May 1999 if no peace accord is reached, raising fears of a confrontation with Israel in those areas. [83]

Then, as CNN reported, out of nowhere, comes the Crown Prince Hassan of Jordan with an "acceptable solution" to both sides. Talks again resumed Thursday, July 23rd.

The significance of Jordan stepping in, as fast as being watchful is concerned is that Jordan per past peace treaties with Israel, maintains control over all of the Muslim holy sights in Israel, including the Temple Mount. They have much to bargain with.

APPENDIX C

The Washington Declaration
Israel - Jordan - The United States
July 25th, 1994

A. After generations of hostility, blood and tears and in the wake of years of pain and wars, His Majesty King Hussein and Prime Minister Yitzhak Rabin are determined to bring an end to bloodshed and sorrow. It is in this spirit that His Majesty King Hussein of the Hashemite Kingdom of Jordan and Prime Minister and Minister of Defense, Mr. Yitzhak Rabin of Israel, met in Washington today at the invitation of President William J. Clinton of the United States of America. This initiative of President William J. Clinton constitutes an historic landmark in the United States' untiring efforts in promoting peace and stability in the Middle East. The personal involvement of the President has made it possible to realise agreement on the content of this historic declaration.
The signing of this declaration bears testimony to the President's vision and devotion to the cause of peace.

B. In their meeting, His Majesty King Hussein and Prime Minister Yitzhak Rabin have jointly reaffirmed the five underlying principles of their understanding on an Agreed Common Agenda designed to reach the goal of a just, lasting and comprehensive peace between the Arab States and the Palestinians, with Israel.
1. Jordan and Israel aim at the achievement of just, lasting and comprehensive peace between Israel and

its neighbours and at the conclusion of a Treaty of Peace between both countries.

2. The two countries will vigorously continue their negotiations to arrive at a state of peace, based on Security Council Resolutions 242 and 338 in all their aspects, and founded on freedom, equality and justice.

3. Israel respects the present special role of the Hashemite Kingdom of Jordan in Muslim Holy shrines in Jerusalem. When negotiations on the permanent status will take place, Israel will give high priority to the Jordanian historic role in these shrines. In addition the two sides have agreed to act together to promote interfaith relations among the three monotheistic religions.

4. The two countries recognise their right and obligation to live in peace with each other as well as with all states within secure and recognised boundaries. The two states affirmed their respect for and acknowledgment of the sovereignty, territorial integrity and political independence of every state in the area.

5. The two countries desire to develop good neighbourly relations of cooperation between them to ensure lasting security and to avoid threats and the use of force between them.

C. The long conflict between the two states is now coming to an end. In this spirit the state of belligerency between Jordan and Israel has been terminated.

D. Following this declaration and in keeping with the Agreed Common Agenda, both countries will refrain from actions or activities by either side that may adversely affect the security of the other or may prejudice the final outcome of negotiations. Neither side will threaten the other by use of force, weapons, or any other means, against each otherm and both sides will thwart threats to security resulting from all kinds of terrorism.

E. His Majesty King Hussein and Prime Minister Yitzhak Rabin took note of the progress made in the bilateral negotiations within the Jordan-Israel track last week on the steps decided to implement the sub- agendas on borders, territorial matters, security, water, energy, environment and the Jordan Rift Valley.

In this framework, mindful of items of the Agreed Common Agenda (borders and territorial matters) they noted that the boundary sub-commission has reached agreement in July 1994 in fulfillment of part of the role entrusted to it in the sub-agenda. They also noted that the sub-commission for water, environment and energy agreed to mutually recognise, as the role of their negotiations, the rightful allocations of the two sides in Jordan River and Yarmouk River waters and to fully respect and comply with the negotiated rightful allocations, in accordance with agreed acceptable principles with mutually acceptable quality. Similarly, His Majesty King Hussein and Prime Minister Yitzhak Rabin expressed their deep satisfaction and pride in the work of the trilateral commission in its meeting held in Jordan on Wednesday, July 20th 1994, hosted by the Jordanian Prime Minister, Dr. Abdessalam al-Majali, and attended by Secretary of State Warren Christopher and Foreign Minister Shimon Peres. They voiced their pleasure at the association and commitment of the United States in this endeavour.

F. His Majesty King Hussein and Prime Minister Yitzhak Rabin believe that steps must be taken both to overcome psychological barriers and to break with the legacy of war. By working with optimism towards the dividends of peace for all the people in the region, Jordan and Israel are determined to shoulder their responsibilities towards the human dimension of peace making. They recognise imbalances and disparities are a root cause of extremism which thrives on poverty and unemployment and the degradation of human dignity. In this spirit His Majesty King Hussein and Prime Minister Yitzhak Rabin have today approved a series of steps to symbolise the new era which is now at hand:

1. Direct telephone links will be opened between Jordan and Israel.

2. The electricity grids of Jordan and Israel will be linked as part of a regional concept.

3. Two new border crossings will be opened between Jordan and Israel - one at the southern tip of Aqaba-Eilat and the other at a mutually agreed point in the north.

4. In principle free access will be given to third country tourists traveling between Jordan and Israel.

5. Negotiations will be accelerated on opening an international air corridor between both countries.

6. The police forces of Jordan and Israel will cooperate in combating crime with emphasis on smuggling and particularly drug smuggling. The United States will be invited to participate in this joint endeavour.

7. Negotiations on economic matters will continue in order to prepare for future bilateral cooperation including the abolition of all economic boycotts.

All these steps are being implemented within the framework of regional infrastructural development plans and in conjunction with the Jordan-Israel bilaterals on boundaries, security, water and related issues and without prejudice to the final outcome of the negotiations on the items included in the Agreed Common Agenda between Jordan and Israel.

G. His Majesty King Hussein and Prime Minister Yitzhak Rabin have agreed to meet periodically or whenever they feel necessary to review the progress of the negotiations and express their firm intention to shepherd and direct the process in its entirety.

H. In conclusion, His Majesty King Hussein and Prime Minister Yitzhak Rabin wish to express once again their profound thanks and appreciation to President William J. Clinton and his Administration for their untiring efforts in furthering the cause of peace, justice and prosperity for all the peoples of the region. They wish to thank the President personally for his warm welcome and hospitality. In recognition of their appreciation to the President, His Majesty King Hussein and Prime Minister Yitzhak Rabin have asked President William J. Clinton to sign this document as a witness and as a host to their meeting.

His Majesty King Hussein
Prime Minister Yitzhak Rabin
President William J. Clinton

FOOTNOTES

1. John Hooper, "*Islam on Probation*," The Guardian, August 7, 1996.
2. ibid.
3. Stanley Cohen, Professor of Criminology, Hebrew University, Jerusalem, <u>Law and Social Inquiry</u>, vol. 20. no. 1, winter, 1995, pp. 7, 50.
4. Walid Shoebat, <u>WHY I LEFT JIHAD</u>, Top Executive Media Publishing, 2005, pp.272-274.
5. ibid., p. 274.
6. Dr. Arnold Fruchtenbaum, "<u>The Footsteps of the Messiah</u>.
7. Dr. John F. Walvoord, <u>Daniel: The Key to Prophetic Revelation</u> (Moody Press), pp. 273-274.
8. Dr. Arnold Fruchtenbaum, "<u>The Footsteps of the Messiah</u>.
9. Walid Shoebat, <u>WHY I LEFT JIHAD</u>, Top Executive Media Publishing, 2005, pp. 318-319.
10. W.E. Vine, "<u>An Expository Dictionary of New Testament Words</u>," Royal Publishers, Nashville, pp. 53-54.
11. Perry A. Stone, "<u>UNLEASHING THE BEAST</u>", Voice of Evangelism, 2003, pp. 19-21.
12. Professor L.L. Cavalli-Sforza, <u>The History and Geography of Human Genes</u>, 1994.
13. ibid.
14. William Dankenbring, "<u>The Mark of Cain</u>"
15. Bill Cloud, "<u>Enmity Between the Seeds</u>," p. 194.
16. Keil, C.F. and Delitzsch F., "Genesis: Commentary on the Old Testament, p. 220.
17. Bill Cloud, "<u>Enmity Between the Seeds</u>," p. 106.
18. Dr. Joe VanKoevering, <u>The Church Under End Time Attack</u>, God's News Publishing, 2002.
19. Walid Shoebat, <u>WHY I LEFT JIHAD</u>, Top Executive Media Publishing, 2005, pp. 320-322.
20. ibid, p. 322.
21. op. cit., p. 372.
22. Perry Stone, Jr., <u>UNLEASHING THE BEAST</u>, Voice of Evangelism, Cleveland, Tennessee, 2003.

23. WND WorldNetDaily.com, January 5, 2007.
24. NEWSWEEK, February 12, 2007, pp.36-37.
25. Hitchcock, Mark, IRAN: THE COMING CRISIS, pp. 71-74.
26. ibid., p. 76.
27. Monetary and Economic Review, Vol. XXI, No. 2, P. 10, "'Smoking Gun': Iranian Weapons in Iraq."
28. Thomas, George, "Inside Iran: Signs of the Apocalypse," CBN News, July 20, 2006.
29. NEWSWEEK interview, August 21, 2006.
30. Knickmeyer, Ellen, WASHINGTON POST article, August 24,2006.
31. Ahmadinejad, Iranian President, U.N. General Assembly speech, September 19, 2006.
32. JERUSALEM POST, January, 2007.
33. Harun Yahya, THE END TIMES AND THE MAHDI, Khatoons Publishing, Maryland, USA, pp. 33-34; 85.
34. Mark Hitchcock, Iran: The Coming Crisis, p. 58.
35. Michael D. Evans, Showdown with Nuclear Iran, Thomas Nelson Publishers, 2006, p.xxiii.
36. DEBKAfile.com.
37. www.clubofrome.org.
38. ibid.
39. Prince El Hassan, speech, before the International Inter-Religious Foundation of the U.K.
40. Prince El Hassan, TO BE A MUSLIM: ISLAM, PEACE, AND DEMOCRACY, Sussex Academic Press, 2004.
41. Prince El Hassan, speech, post 9/11, www.elhassan.org.
42. ibid.
43. THE JERUSALEM POST.
44. DAILY STAR "Is it Prince Hassan's Moment?"
45. Michael Rubin, "If Iraqis Want a King, Hassan of Jordan Could Be Their Man," 2002.
46. Professor Abdulaziz Sachedina, Jewish World News, December 23, 2004.
47. FORWARD NEWS, "Jordan Prince Said to Seek Iraqi Throne."

48. ibid.
49. ECONOMIST, *"A King for Iraq?"*
50. C NEWS, *"Jordan's Prince Hassan Raises Concern – He's looking for a kingdom - in Iraq."*
51. JORDAN TIMES, *"Iraqi Religious Leaders Call for Immediate Interim Government,"* May 20, 2003.
52. ibid.
53. Brian Whitaker, *"A Prince Coming to the Aid of Babylon (Iraq),"* THE GUARDIAN UNLIMITED.
54. ibid.
55. David Pryce-Jones, *"A time for Kings? Hashemites and other in the Arab mix,"* NATIONAL REVIEW, September 2, 2002.
56. Michael Freeland, *"The man who could be King,"* THE GUARDIAN UNLIMITED, 2003.
57. ibid.
58. David Ignatius, *"Is it Prince Hassan's moment?"* the DAILY STAR, December 1, 2004.
59. BBC News Report , *"Who's who in post Saddam Iraq,"* April 15, 2003.
60. Khalees Times Online, *"Prince Hassan ready to play a role in Iraq,"* April 6, 2003.
61. enews World, Jamal Halaby.
62. Michael Rubin, *"If Iraqis want a King, Hassan could be their man,"* 2002.
63. Adeed I. Dawisha and Karen Dawisha, FOREIGN AFFAIRS, *"How to Build a Democratic Iraq,"* May/June 2003.
64. Bernard Lewis and James Woolsey, *"After the War: King and Country, The Hashemite solution for Iraq,"* WALL STREET JOURNAL, October 29, 2003.
65. Late Majesty King Hussein, personal correspondence to his younger brother, his Royal Highness Prince El Hassan, January 25th, 1999.
66. Helio Fred Garcia, *"Harnessing Religions in Pursuit of Peace,"* UN-World, May/June, 2004.
67. JERUSALEM POST, October 29th, 2004.
68. Prince El Hassan, "A Study on Jerusalem", 1978.
69. Prince El Hassan, speech, New School University in New York,

a forum entitled, *"A Muslim Centrist Platform for Democracy in the Arab World,"* sponsored by "Dialogues," January 28, 2004.

70. Ruth Lapidot, Israel Ministry of Foreign Affairs, *"Jerusalem."*

71. *"Jordanian Policy on Jerusalem,"* Jordanian official website

72. Prime Minister Abd al-Salin al-Majali, *"As to what the final solution will be, there will be a role for Jordan in any final solution,"* MBC, October 30, 1994. Also see www.elhassan.org.

73. ibid.

74. Joel C. Rosenberg, *"TWELFTH IMAM COULD APPEAR THIS SPRING, SAYS IRAN!"* WASHINGTON, D.C., January 2, 2007.

75. Prince El Hassan, speech, Club of Rome appointment, 2000.

76. Jerusalem Report Magazine's 10th Anniversary, interview with Prince El Hassan, 1992.

77. Prince El Hassan, A Study on Jerusalem, 1978.

78. Prince Hassan, speech, European-Atlantic Group, November 20, 2003.

79. Marshall J. Broger and Thomas A. Idinopulos, Policy Paper Series NO. 46 Washington, D.C.: The Washington Institute for Near East Policy, 1998.

80. Clement Henry, *"Profile of Prince Hassan,"* November 21, 1996.

81. Joan Van Wessel, Jerusalem Report.

82. www.kingabdullah.jo

83. *FOXNEWS*, Jerusalem News Conference, Labor lawmaker Yossi Beilin, 1999.

BIBLIOGRAPHY

BOOKS

Bloomfield, Arthur E., THE END OF THE DAYS.

Cavalli-Sforza, Professor L.L., The History and Geography of Human Genes, 1994.

Cloud, Bill, Enmity Between the Seeds, 2006

Dankenbring, William, The Mark of Cain.

El Hassan, Prince, A STUDY OF JERUSALEM, Longman (London and New York), in association with the Publishing Committee, Amman, Jordan, 1978.

El Hassan, Prince, CHRISTIANITY IN THE ARAB WORLD, Continium Press, (New York, Great Britain), 1995 and 1998.

El Hassan, Prince, TO BE A MUSLIM: ISLAM, PEACE, AND DEMOCRACY, Sussex Academic Press, 2004.

Evans, Michael D., Showdown with Nuclear Iran, Thomas Nelson Publishers, Nashville, Tennessee, 2006.

Fruchtenbaum, Arnold, The Footsteps of the Messiah.

Hitchcock, Mark, Iran: The Coming Crisis, (Multnomah Press).

Keil, C.F. and Delitzsch F., Genesis: Commentary on the Old Testament.

Shoebat, Walid, WHY I LEFT JIHAD, Top Executive Media Publishing, 2005.

Stone, Perry Jr., UNLEASHING THE BEAST, Voice of Evangelism, Cleveland, Tennessee, 2003.

VanKoevering, Joe, The Church Under End Time Attack, God's News Publishing, 2002.

Vine, W.E., An Expository Dictionary of New Testament Words, Royal Publishers, Nashville.

Walvoord, John F., Daniel: The Key to Prophetic Revelation (Moody Press).

Yahya, Harun, THE END TIMES AND THE MAHDI, Khatoons Publishing, Maryland, March, 2004.

JOURNALS OR MAGAZINES

Abd al-Salin al-Majali, Prime Minister, *"As to what the final solution will be, there will be a role for Jordan in any final solution,"* MBC, October 30, 1994.

Broger, Marchall J. and Thomas A. Idinopulos, Policy Paper Series NO. 46 Washington, D.C.: The Washington Institute for Near East Policy, 1998.

C NEWS, *"Jordan's Prince Hassan Raises Concern – He's looking for a kingdom - in Iraq."*

Cohen, Stanley, Professor of Criminology, Hebrew University, Jerusalem, Law and Social Inquiry, vol. 20. no. 1, winter, 1995, pp. 7, 50.

Davis, Douglas, *"Prince Hassan tells 'Post' he seeks Mideast peace,"* FINANCIAL TIMES, via Jerusalem Post, October 28, 2004.

Dawisha, Adeed I. and Karen, FOREIGN AFFAIRS, *"How to Build a Democratic Iraq,"* May/June 2003.

ECONOMIST, *"A King for Iraq?"*

enews World, Jamal Halaby.

FORWARD NEWS, *"Jordan Prince Said to Seek Iraqi Throne."*

Freeland, Michael, *"The man who could be King,"* THE GUARDIAN UNLIMITED, 2003.

Helio Fred Garcia, *"Harnessing Religions in Pursuit of Peace,"* UN-World, May/June, 2004.

Henry, Clement, *"Profile of Prince Hassan,"* November 21, 1996.

Hooper, John, *"Islam on Probation,"* The Guardian, August 7, 1996.

Hussein, Late Majesty King, personal correspondence to his younger brother, his Royal Highness Prince El Hassan, January 25th, 1999.

Ignatius, David, *"Is it Prince Hassan's moment?"* the DAILY STAR, December 1, 2004.

JERUSALEM POST, January, 2007.

JERUSALEM POST, October 29th, 2004.

Jerusalem Report Magazine's 10th Anniversary, interview with Prince El Hassan, 1992.

Jervis, Rick, *"Hard-won turf easily lost in transfer to Iraqis,"* USA TODAY, October 30, 2006, p. 10A.

JORDAN TIMES, *"Iraqi Religious Leaders Call for Immediate Interim Government,"* May 20, 2003.

Khalees Times Online, *"Prince Hassan ready to play a role in Iraq,"* April 6, 2003.

Knickmeyer, Ellen, WASHINGTON POST article, August 24, 2006.

Lapidot, Ruth, Israel Ministry of Foreign Affairs, *"Jerusalem."*

Lewis, Bernard and James Woolsey, *"After the War: King and Country, The Hashemite solution for Iraq,"* WALL STREET JOURNAL, October 29, 2003.

Monetary and Economic Review, Vol. XXI, No. 2, P. 10, " *'Smoking Gun': Iranian Weapons in Iraq."*

NEWSWEEK interview, August 21, 2006.

NEWSWEEK, February 12, 2007.

NEWSWEEK, September 25, 2006.

Pryce-Jones, David, *"A time for Kings? Hashemites and other in the Arab mix,"* NATIONAL REVIEW, September 2, 2002.

Rosenberg, Joel C., *"TWELFTH IMAM COULD APPEAR THIS SPRING, SAYS IRAN!"* WASHINGTON, D.C., January 2, 2007.

Rubin, Michael, *"If Iraqis Want a King, Hassan of Jordan Could Be Their Man,"* 2002.

Sachedina, Professor Abdulaziz, Jewish World News, December 23, 2004.

Thomas, George, *"Inside Iran: Signs of the Apocalypse,"* CBN News, July 20, 2006.

Van Wessel, Joan, Jerusalem Report.

Whitaker, Brian, *"A Prince Coming to the Aid of Babylon (Iraq),"* THE GUARDIAN UNLIMITED.

ZEW'S NEWS REVIEW, "The Jesus Challenge," Issue 109, November 12, 2006.

MEDIAS

BBC News Report , *"Who's who in post Saddam Iraq,"* April 15, 2003.

FOXNEWS, Jerusalem News Conference, Labor lawmaker Yossi Beilin, 1999.

SPEECHES

Ahmadinejad, Iranian President, U.N. General Assembly, September 19, 2006.

Prince Hassan, European-Atlantic Group, November 20, 2003.

Prince El Hassan, International Inter-Religious Foundation of the U.K.

Prince El Hassan, Iraqi Religious Leaders Convene to Address Growing Sectarianism as One-Year Anniversary Approaches, March 10-12, 2004, Amman, Jordan.

Prince El Hassan, New School University in New York, a forum entitled, *"A Muslim Centrist Platform for Democracy in the Arab World,"* sponsored by "Dialogues," January 28, 2004.

Prince El Hassan, speech, post 9/11, www.elhassan.org.

Prince El Hassan, Club of Rome appointment, 2000.

Prince El Hassan, "Waging war or winning peace," July 27, 2006, www.haaretz.com.

WEBSITES

www.clubofrome.org

www.cultureofpeaceexhibit.org

DEBKAfile.com

www.elhassan.org

www.financialtimes.com

www.kingabdullah.jo

MSNBC.com, Knickmeyer, Ellen, "*'Shiite giant' extends its reach,*" via THE WASHIGNTON POST, August 24, 2006.

MSNBC.com, Knickmeyer, Ellen, *"Mahdi Army brings slaughter to the streets,"* via THE WASHINGTON POST, August 25, 2006.

MSNBC.com, THE ASSOCIATED PRESS, *"Assad to U.S.: Work with Syuria on Iraq,"* February 5, 2007.

MSNBC.com, THE ASSOCAITED PRESS, *"Iran's leader warns U.S. against attack,"* February 8, 2007.

www.tanenbaum.org

WND WorldNetDaily.com, January 5, 2007.

I trust this book has been informational, inspirational, challenging, and motivational to you, to assist you to **"BE READY** *for in such a time as this, the Son of Man cometh!"*

Be sure to contact us, and look at our website for additional Biblical prophecy information and books at: **www.godsnews.com**

Write us today at:

**Dr. Joe VanKoevering
God's News Behind the News
P.O. Box 10475
St. Petersburg, FL 33733
U.S.A.**

1-800-366-1463